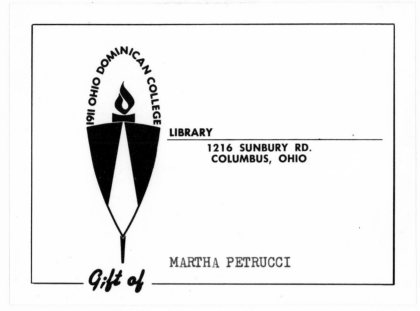

# COAL
## THE ROCK THAT BURNS

# COAL

## THE ROCK THAT BURNS

Walter Harter

Elsevier/Nelson Books
New York

Copyright © 1979 by Walter Harter

**Library of Congress Cataloging in Publication Data**

Harter, Walter L
  Coal: the rock that burns.

  Includes index.
  SUMMARY: Describes coal, where it's found, how it's recovered, who mines it, and its many uses.
  1. Coal—Juvenile literature. [1. Coal.
2. Coal mines and mining] I. Title.
TN801.H18     553'.2     78-27745
ISBN 0-525-66609-2

Published in the United States by Elsevier/Nelson Books, a division of Elsevier-Dutton Publishing Company, Inc., New York. Published simultaneously in Don Mills, Ontario, by Thomas Nelson and Sons (Canada) Limited.

Printed in the U.S.A.     First Edition
10  9  8  7  6  5  4  3  2  1

*For Martin Marschang*
*in appreciation of his friendship and help.*

# Contents

# About This Book

For a little while coal was almost forgotten. Other fuels—solar energy, nuclear energy, and, of course, oil—were more popular.

But the growing population and its increasing need for energy have prompted scientists in both government and industry to examine more fully our current and future energy requirements, especially since oil is becoming scarce and ever more expensive.

The possibilities of energy from the sun are fantastic. But only a small amount of research and experimentation has been done. The same is true of wind and thermal sources of power. Nuclear energy, too, has tremendous potential. But so far the dangers connected with it have outnumbered its blessings.

Oil seemed to fill all the requirements for energy and for a long list of by-products that have made our lives easier and longer. But oil has one important drawback: its reserves are dwindling. It is estimated that the once huge underground pools of oil will be drained within the next twenty or thirty years, certainly within the life span of many people alive today.

Coal reserves, on the other hand, are believed to total more than *five thousand million tons,* and could supply the world's energy needs for the next four centuries. The United States alone has coal deposits that should last this country for two thousand years.

More useful things can be made from coal than from oil. For not only are there some things that can be made *only* from coal, but oil itself, with all its many by-products, can be obtained from coal. Even gasoline can be manufactured from coal at a cost of approximately ten cents a gallon.

Manufacturing gasoline from coal is not new. During World War II the Luftwaffe, the Nazi air force, used only gasoline made from coal. The process was expensive then, but the Germans needed gasoline, no matter the cost. New methods have made that process cheaper and more logical.

During the reign of oil, coal was not completely forgotten. Research has gone on steadily to make it more satisfactory and useful. Ways have been discovered to remove the pollutants that occur when some kinds of coal are burned. New methods of mining have been developed, so that coal can be dug from the earth at lower cost and in greater amounts. And many new products, such as better medicines and various plastics, can now be made from it.

In the future we will, of course, use oil, solar, and nuclear energies when possible. But we now know that in "the rock that burns" we have an ensured supply not only of energy, but of chemical wonders that will make our civilization healthier and more secure.

The story of coal—how it was formed so many millions of years ago, how it was discovered, and how it has been used and will be used—makes a fascinating tale.

# 1 "The Rocks Are Burning!"

### THE LONG HUNTERS

The two hunters made camp early. The beaver traps they had planted in various streams throughout this wilderness area of western Pennsylvania had yielded a good catch. The October night was starry and crisp, and promised a clear day for more trapping.

Their small campfire was built in a nest of stones. "Lew" Wenzel, the older of the two men, squatted close to the flames, mending a tear in his buckskin leggings. Henry Webb, his companion, came from the surrounding forest, carrying more wood.

Webb stopped and stared. "Lew, look!"

The older man dropped flat to the ground and reached for his rifle. Years of wandering in the wilds had made him alert to every danger. "What? Where?" His eyes scanned the trees that loomed over the camp.

Webb dropped the wood he was carrying and pointed to the fire. *"The rocks are burning!"*

Wenzel turned quickly and stared at the fire. The stones against which the wood was burning *were* glowing and sputtering. He also felt a strange heat, stronger heat than usually came from a wood fire.

"It's the spirits!" he whispered. "I've seen 'em before. Likely we've camped on an old Indian burial ground, and they want us out o' here!"

To the hunters and trappers who wandered through the wilds of our country in early days, "spirits" were real and important. Living so close to nature, they had experienced many strange things, things that could be explained to their simple minds only by believing in the ghosts of the dead.

The two trappers quickly poured water on their fire and moved their camp a few miles away.

Of course the "burning rocks" were parts of an outcrop of bituminous coal on which they had built their campfire. This type of coal is also called soft coal, and it lies close to the surface of the earth in many parts of the world. Wind and rain expose it, and it is easily set ablaze by campfires or lightning. There are many legends about how patches of "burning earth" have made people in the distant past fear they were seeing omens of destruction and catastrophe.

### The Discovery of Anthracite

But there is another important type of coal, one that is seldom exposed accidentally. Lying deep in the ground, it is difficult to mine, but it is the most valuable and therefore the most sought after of the different kinds of coal. This is the so-called hard coal, or anthracite.

The year was 1812. England and the young United States were at war, and the new democracy was being made defenseless by a naval blockade.

Americans had learned from their experience in the Revolutionary War how important it was to be able to manufacture their own iron and other metal products. During the years of peace, small factories had been set up, and brawny patriots had put them into operation.

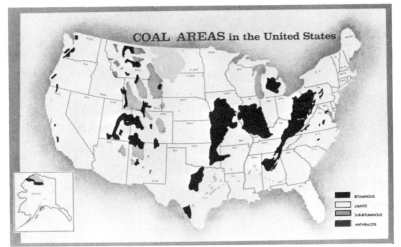

COAL AREAS in the United States

*National Coal Association*

But the mills and forges were dependent on one basic thing—something to burn in the furnaces to supply heat. Wood had been their first fuel and was still used. But after the discovery of soft coal, even with its drawbacks of stench and smoke, the furnaces of the young country had come to depend on the easily mined black stones.

Bituminous coal had been carted to the small factories by farmers who earned extra cash for an easily harvested crop of coal lying on their fields. But as more and more mills were built, the need for coal became so great it was imported from England.

In the years immediately preceding 1812, the wharves of New York and Philadelphia had been piled high with tons and tons of bituminous coal, waiting to be loaded on wagons and transported to iron mills and blast furnaces. And new outcroppings of great size had been discovered in Virginia. Ships left the ports of that state every day loaded with bituminous coal, bound for mills in the North.

But now there was war. And because of that war the

British had placed a tight naval blockade along the American East Coast. Vessels from England, heavily laden with soft coal, were turned back, and American coastal ships were locked in southern harbors. Some attempts were made to send the coal north by wagons, but the roads between the states were impassable to all but lone horsemen. Even if the roads had been in good condition, there weren't enough wagons to carry the required tonnage to supply the northern forges and ironworks.

So wood was used again. Whole forests were cut down. But it required huge quantities of it to create enough heat to manufacture metals. Soon wood became scarce, then not available at all. Large parts of our great land were, of course, still covered with trees, but no longer were forests within a reasonable distance of where wood was needed.

One by one the roaring fires in the small ironworks began to go out. Even Thomas Jefferson shut down his small nail factory at Monticello. The United States would soon be at the mercy of any country that could produce more and better metal.

Then, one day in June of 1814, a line of ten wagons creaked over rutted roads across the hills of Delaware County in Pennsylvania. Each wagon was dragged by four oxen. Piled high against the wooden sides were rocks that appeared to be brown in the slanting sunlight.

The man who rode his horse at the head of the procession was named Shoemaker. The merchandise he carried in his ten wagons helped the United States keep its independence, and started an age of industrialization in the United States.

What Mr. Shoemaker had for sale was coal—hard coal, anthracite. Of course he wasn't quite certain what he had discovered on his farm. It didn't look like the familiar black coal, and it had a strange hardness. It hadn't been lying on the surface of his fields, either. In fact, he'd had to hire some men to dig deep into the ground for enough to fill the ten wagons. And it wasn't easy to ignite. But when it did burn it gave off great heat and little smoke.

Mr. Shoemaker and his wagons traveled until they came to an ironworks near Philadelphia. There he asked the price of $40 a ton for his brown rocks, claiming it had cost him $28 for labor to dig each ton.

The owner of the furnace, Josiah White, hesitated. Bituminous coal cost only a few dollars a ton, even though it was transported from England or Virginia. But there was no bituminous coal, so he decided to take a chance. He would have bought anything that would feed the fires in his furnace.

The brown fuel did burn, and it did produce a fierce heat. Soon Mr. Shoemaker was supplying anthracite coal to every mill he could reach with his wagons.

When other men began to search for hard coal, they discovered that Mr. Shoemaker's farm lay at the southern tip of one of the largest deposits of anthracite coal in the world. Huge buried masses of that valuable fuel extended far into the north of the state. In time the deep mines of central and northeastern Pennsylvania produced, and still produce, most of the energy for what have become the immense steel mills of today.

### COAL IN ANCIENT TIMES

Coal was being used long before the two hunters saw it burning in their campfire.

The Chinese used coal three thousand years ago to smelt iron and copper. Marco Polo wrote that the most memorable of his experiences during his twenty years of wandering in strange places was watching Chinese use "the rock that burns."

Excavations in many parts of England have exposed coal cinders beneath ancient Roman towns, proving that those conquerors knew about coal. There is written proof, too, that the Anglo-Saxons used coal long before the Norman invasion. The Saxon chronicle of the Abbey of Peterborough, dated A.D. 872, two hundred years before the battle of Hastings, relates that Abbot Coelred rented some land to a man called Wulfred, who was to deliver to the abbey each year "60 loads of wood, 12 loads of coal, and 6 loads of peat."

In Europe those who did know about coal used it, especially the poor, who found it cheaper than wood to heat their cottages.

The rich preferred to burn wood in their mansions and castles, claiming it was unhealthy to breathe the smoke of coal and that food cooked over it was poisonous. What was mostly available then, of course, was bituminous coal, which does smoke and smell unpleasant.

In the Western Hemisphere, the Hopi Indians are thought to have been the first users of coal. Deposits at their ancient campsites show that they used it in the manufacture of pottery as far back as the eleventh century.

Most of the early users of coal knew only the soft kind. Bituminous coal was easier to mine because it lay on or just below the surface of the earth. Anthracite was rare and precious to those Europeans who knew it, and in the United States it was almost unknown. Very rarely did the top of a vein penetrate the surface of the ground, and when that small piece was used up, it required hard labor to dig out more coal from the earth. Also, the more primitive the people were, the more reluctant they were to work underground in the primeval darkness of a mine.

As our country developed over the past two hundred years, so did the coal industry. Inventive minds created easier and less expensive methods of bringing coal to the surface. Veins of commerce—the canals, roads, and railways—came to link all parts of the country, so that everyone, everywhere, could make use of nature's black gold.

## A GLANCE INTO COAL'S FUTURE

For thousands of years coal was used only as a substitute for wood, and no one knew of the wonders that lay hidden in each small piece. But in the past hundred years, and especially in the last fifty, the humble black mineral has spawned marvel after marvel. And new ones continue to appear.

Large quantities of coal are still being used as fuel. Industry needs tremendous amounts, and many houses are heated by burning coal. Coal is also used to generate electricity, and scientists have found methods of manufacturing gas and oil from it.

And from these new uses of coal have evolved dozens of other fuels—light and heavy oils of all kinds, tars, and many chemical compounds. But probably the greatest benefits derived from coal are in the field of medicine. New drugs and remedies have been developed from coal, and old medicines have been made less expensive.

Unlocking the mysteries and wonders of coal is like exploring a wilderness only partly mapped. For coal is truly a dark continent, a vast area of many undiscovered secrets.

The story of coal begins approximately 300 million years ago, when the first living things began to breathe a mixture of air and water in the dense forests of the Paleozoic era.

# 2 How the Deposits of Coal Were Formed

THE GEOLOGICAL AGES

To understand how the immense coal beds were made, it is necessary to know something of the earth's history.

The age of our world is roughly divided into four principal periods of time. The Precambrian Era is the oldest. It began two or three *billion* years ago, when there was no life on the earth at all, and at its conclusion only worms and one-celled plants lived in the warm seas. Then came the Paleozoic Era, beginning about half a billion years in the past, during which dense forests flourished on the land that had emerged from the oceans. Next was the Mesozoic Era, about 190 million years ago, when dinosaurs appeared and then became extinct. Finally there is the Cenozoic Era, beginning 60 million years in the past and including the present time.

The billions and millions of years might be better understood if we remember that *time,* as it is thought of in geology, is *slow.* We could stand and stare at the

Rocky Mountains, day after day, week after week, and notice no change. Yet in a billion years that same mountain range could have been raised to its greatest height and eroded down to the level of the sea *one hundred and sixty-five times!*

Or here's another example: The Empire State Building in New York City soars into the sky to a height of 1,472 feet. If one dime were to be placed on its highest point, it could represent the length of time men have walked erect upon the earth. The height of the building itself would then represent the time elapsed since the beginning of the Precambrian Era.

In three billion years the earth has gone through many changes. Its crust has buckled and wrinkled up into mountain ranges, then been worn down level again, many times and in many places. Our great plains are really the bottoms of ancient seas. Some are a billion years old, but others are "young," having appeared only a few million years ago.

Even now the earth is changing beneath our feet. Immense pressures are being exerted on it from its core, which is still fiery hot. Instruments tell us of the dozens of earthquakes and tremors that shake the earth's surface every day. The movements of the tides erode our seacoasts daily, causing some coastal areas to shrink and others to emerge from the sea, creating new land. The action never stops.

The rocks of our mountains are composed of sandstones, limestones, and shale, the same as those found on the bottom of the ocean. Mixed with these are igneous rocks—fire-formed rocks that have come from inside the earth in molten form and then hardened. Great pressures are needed to squeeze new rocks up from the fiery interior of the earth.

The many theories about the birth of our earth seem to agree that it is made up of different masses of material, all moving in a rotating manner. Some of these masses are heavy, others light. The heavy masses slowly sink, pushing up the lighter ones. Since the earth was created, these heavy and light masses have slowly shifted and settled, raising continents and mountain ranges, and allowing other parts of the world to sink and create seas and oceans.

There is a theory that at one time North America and Europe were one, and that they were torn apart by immense pressures as the masses shifted. In the same way the shapes of other continents have changed, as the light and heavy parts of the world rose and fell.

Therefore it is necessary to regard our earth not as solid and enduring, but as something that is shifting and moving every second of every day. Our moving home is very different from what it was millions of years ago. And if we could see its physical shape millions of years in the future, that would be unrecognizable to us also.

### FOSSILS

Fossils help tell us the story of the earth's great age. "The book that never ends," one ancient Chinese philosopher called them.

Exactly what are fossils? Originally the word meant any mineral or rock that had been taken from the earth. Now it means the *remains* or *impression* of any plant or animal life that is found imbedded in rocks.

In the sixteenth century, George Bauer (who translated his name into Latin as Georgius Agricola), the father of modern mineralogy, gave the name to these objects of the distant past. It is from the Latin word *fossus,* and means "dug up."

Many men in the past have studied the stories fossils tell. Herodotus, the fifth-century B.C. Greek historian, was interested in fossils he found along the Nile River. But he finally came to the conclusion that they were only bits and pieces of things discarded by the slaves who had built the Pyramids.

It was a sixth-century A.D. Greek physician, Alexan-

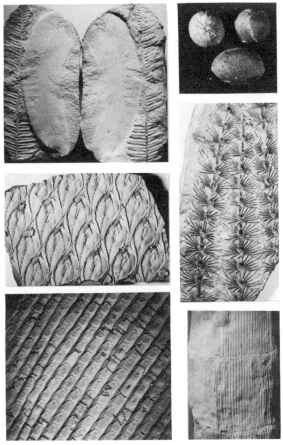

Fossils or impressions of plants that grew in the swampy forests of the Pennsylvania Period (300 million years ago) are often found in and around coal seams. Left, from top to bottom: a single pinnule from the leaf of *Neuropteris* and a pinna from the leaf of *Pecopteris;* an impression from the stem of *Lepidodendron,* the scale tree, showing points of leaf attachment; an impression of the stem of *Siqillaria,* the seal tree, showing points of leaf attachment. Right, from top to bottom: fossil plant seeds of the genus *Triqonocarpus;* leafy branches of the genus *Asterophyllites,* a part of the giant horsetail; cast of the stem of the giant horsetail.

*The Smithsonian Institution*

der of Tralles, who really began to understand their meaning. He was especially fascinated by the fossils of fishes, and, amazingly, he taught that man had descended from creatures of the sea.

Leonardo da Vinci was the first to begin to understand the true story that fossils had to tell. He spent much time exploring the high mountains of Italy. The fossils he discovered during his journeys convinced him that these mountains were not the remnants of the biblical Flood, as was thought at that time, but were the bottoms of seas that had been raised to great heights by the convulsions of the earth.

Fossils tell another story, too. They show that there were forms of life in the past that are not on earth today. Some of that extinct life could not exist today, and a great many of the creatures now alive could not have lived on the earth as it was then.

New discoveries of fossils are helping scientists in their search for the answer to the earth's beginnings. Of course all of it adds up to one thing—time. Time for continents to rise and fall. Time for seas to become mountaintops and mountains to become ocean beds. Time was needed for the slow dance of the earth's crust to crush and compress the dead plant life of the Carboniferous Period into coal.

### THE CARBONIFEROUS PERIOD

The earth's four main time periods each have many subdivisions. The Carboniferous Period was only one part of the Paleozoic Era. But it was during that time that coal began to be formed.

Then the earth was mostly swamps filled with plants that flourished in a moist and humid climate. It was a world of greenery. Sunlight poured down, giving the plants energy for rapid growth. Ferns covered most of the world then—some varieties only an inch long, others towering eighty feet into the warm air.

The climate was tropical. Fishes and insects were the only forms of animal life. There were no birds, butterflies, or bees, for the plants bore no flowers. Toward the end of the Paleozoic Era other forms of life, especially reptiles, began to appear. But in this particular period it was as if nature hesitated for a time to concentrate on laying the foundations for the energy we would use 300 million years later.

The Carboniferous Age is often called the Pennsylvania Period, for it was during those years that the largest layers of coal were formed in the eastern part of that state, especially anthracite.

The process is fascinating. As the huge plants died, they fell into the warm waters of the swamps. Layer upon layer became saturated and sank. Then fungi and bacteria began their work of decomposition.

The first layer of decomposing plant life is called peat, and nature is continuously making it in various parts of the world. Some of it will be the foundations of other coal beds, to be mined by our descendants millions of years in the future.

The decomposing masses of dead plant life, buried one layer upon another, were gradually transformed by immense pressures into lignite, or brown coal, then into bituminous coal, and finally into anthracite.

Scientists have proved that it required twenty feet of compressed plant remains to make one foot of coal. To quote one authority on the Pennsylvania coalfields:

> Many forests would have to grow and die, fall and decay, to produce so thick a deposit. When it is realized that in some parts of the anthracite region of Pennsylvania there are as many as twenty beds of coal having an average thickness of 154 feet, it isn't difficult to conceive of the millions of years necessary to form the anthracite coalfields.

### CHANGES IN COAL BEDS

The process of carbonization is simply the action of heat and pressure on decaying plant material. According to one of America's leading geologists:

There can be no doubt that anthracite coal was caused by "the folding of the areas." In Pennsylvania and other places, where the crust of the earth has folded most (making mountains) there is the hardest coal. When there was less folding, the coal is softer.

Once it was thought that only time was the cause of the hardness of coal. Time *is* important, but now geologists believe that pressure is the most important factor. There are some bituminous beds that are much older than neighboring beds of anthracite. But more pressures had been exerted on the younger beds, making the coal harder.

The heat of molten rocks can cause changes in beds of coal. The liquid rock, squeezed up from deep inside the earth, can penetrate coal veins, altering the type of coal. This has happened often in German coalfields, where shafts of basalt have been forced completely through veins of coal. This coal then becomes red-brown and brittle, and loses its quality.

Coal is also sometimes changed by underground streams. If the water is pure, it can improve the quality of the coal. But often the water is filled with impurities. Impure water, washing over and through the beds, deposit minerals like ash and iron, and reduces the quality.

Another danger to coal beds is spontaneous combustion. Fires are often started deep underground by heat caused by the pressures. If the coal is damp because of underground streams and has absorbed quantities of oxygen, it can ignite and burn for many years.

Some coal beds have smoldered for a long time. In some places, especially in Germany, the heat from burning beds deep in the earth has warmed the ground for hundreds of years. The evidences of old coal-bed fires are seen everywhere in extensive coalfields. The surrounding rocks have been baked into many shades of red, yellow, and blue.

Subterranean rivers sometimes cause coal beds to sink. If the force of the rushing water is strong enough, it will wash away the underlying stone, shale, and gravel, and the entire bed will fall. That is why veins of coal sometimes run in a straight line for a considerable distance, then suddenly plunge to a deeper level. Often the underground streams that caused this phenomenon have long since died or changed their courses. The pressures on these fallen beds may turn bituminous coal into anthracite.

### Strange Things Found in Coal Beds

Gases of various kinds, principally carbon dioxide, methane, and nitrogen, are found in coal of all types. Usually the harder the coal is, the greater quantities of captured gases it will contain. With modern methods these gases can be separated from the coal and used for many purposes.

In bituminous beds methane, or marsh gas, is quite frequent and dangerous. When it becomes mixed with air, it forms firedamp, a dangerous gas that causes many mine explosions. If there is little or no ventilation in a mine, the methane accumulates and, mixing with carbon dioxide, explodes. The danger of explosion increases if the vein has faults—that is, fissures caused by the action of underground water that cause the vein to break and sink. Gases fill the vacuum, and suddenly, there is an explosion.

Coal dust can cause explosions, too, when various other factors are present. The dust formed by drilling, blasting, cutting, loading, and hauling can drift into pockets and explode.

Many strange things are found in coal beds. Some of the most fascinating are called coal pebbles. These are round pieces of coal, which can be picked from a vein like nuts from shells. They vary in size from a few inches to several feet. No one has been able to explain exactly how coal pebbles are formed.

Some geologists claim the pebbles are pieces of peat that have been rounded by the action of wind and rain on the shores of ancient bogs, and that the larger pebbles could be the trunks of trees that have been acted on in the same way. But mostly the pebbles remain a mystery. Some of the finest examples are in coal museums throughout the world.

Animal remains are often found in coal beds, too. These, although ancient, are not true fossils, but have been preserved almost in their original condition, particularly teeth, bones, and skulls. Sometimes shells of a startling whiteness are found in a vein of coal. They, of course, came from oceans that washed over the plant material as it was decomposing. But why they are in perfect condition is a mystery.

Peat, too, can preserve some extraordinary things. In Denmark, in May 1950, men cutting up a peat bog were astounded to see a foot and leg protruding from a cut they had just made. Careful excavation disclosed a man lying on his side, curled up as though asleep. He wore only a cap and belt. Around his neck were two leather thongs that had choked him to death. The skin was like parchment, except that it had turned the dark-brown color of the peat that had preserved it. His features were as well preserved as those of a man only a few hours dead.

Had he been murdered? Had he been executed? Had he been sacrificed for religious reasons? No one can be sure. Whatever the reason for his death, it happened approximately two thousand years ago. The seven-foot layer of peat that covered his body proved it had been placed in the bog that long ago.

Another mystery to geologists is the presence of rocks and even boulders in coal beds. They have been found in various sizes, from less than an inch in diameter to one discovered in an Ohio mine that weighed four hundred pounds. The latter is now in a museum in Columbus.

These rocks and boulders are composed mostly of quartz. One theory for their presence is that they were held in the roots of the plants that formed the coal. But that doesn't explain some of the huge rocks found, especially the one in Ohio, which would be too large to be held in plant roots.

A strange thing about the rocks is that most of them don't come from the same stratum as that of the basic plant material that made the coal. Radioactive tests of the plant life compressed in them prove that they predate the Carboniferous Age—that is, they existed before the coal they are hidden in was formed. The pressure needed to process the coal should have pulverized the rocks. Yet they show no damage at all.

Another mystery about coal is why common charcoal is found, to some degree, in all types of true coal. Miners don't like charcoal. It not only lowers the quality of the vein, but contributes to the amount of dust in a mine, therefore adding to the danger of explosions.

The charcoal found in coal seams has a bright, silky luster. It rubs off easily, and very often can be "peeled," showing the age rings of the wood from which it was made.

Charcoal is the result of the almost complete burning of wood. Commercial charcoal is manufactured in kilns, but forest fires can accomplish the same thing. The charcoal found in coal beds today *could* be the result of ancient forest fires that were started by lightning or volcanic action, but not all geologists agree. Writes one specialist:

> The argument against that is that the tremendous amounts of charcoal sometimes found in coal seams could be the result only of almost continuous forest fires in ancient times. And the moist condition of the Carboniferous forests makes it difficult to believe that fires of any great size could have occurred at that time.

These are only a few of the mysteries about coal, mysteries that lie in the veins for us to see and puzzle over.

However, the real mysteries that are hidden *in* coal can be discovered only by methods of modern research.

An ancient man, holding a black rock in his hand, could never imagine that oil, gas, medicines, and hundreds of other wonders were hidden in it—just as modern scientists are still unaware of the additional marvels that are waiting to be discovered in the rock that burns.

But they know they are there. And the search for them goes on, day after day. One by one the riddles hidden in coal are being solved for the benefit of mankind.

# 3 Different Kinds of Coal and Their Uses

A diamond is the hardest substance known. It is 100 percent pure carbon, and made by volcanic pressure. Coal also contains carbon, which is why the geological age in which it was formed is called the *Carboniferous Period*. But coal is made by various other pressures, plus time.

It is the amount of carbon in coal that determines its hardness. Here is a list of coals and the amounts of carbon they contain:

Anthracite  ..........................95 percent
Bituminous coal  .....................82 percent
Lignite ..............................69 percent
Peat  ................................59 percent

"Anthracite" comes from a Greek word, *anthrax,* "coal." It was used by a student of Aristotle, the Greek philosopher, in an article he wrote on stones about 370 B.C. In the article he mentioned fossil substances "that are called coals, which kindle and burn." This is probably the first recorded mention of true coal.

When anthracite burns, it produces almost no smoke, and its heat is intense. For that reason it sells for a higher price than bituminous coal.

Anthracite is broken up at the mine into various sizes, ranging from "broken," averaging five inches in size, through "egg," "pea," and "buckwheat," which is only approximately 3/64th of an inch in diameter. "Rice" and "barley," both smaller than "buckwheat," are used chiefly in automatic stokers in hotels and office buildings. "Egg" and "pea" coal are the size used most often in heating private houses.

Since the mining of anthracite began, more than 160 years ago, most of it has been used in home furnaces. However, since gas, oil, and electricity became popular, that use has slowly dwindled. And it has almost disappeared from public buildings.

However, the iron-and-steel industries have continued to use great amounts of anthracite, especially to manufacture things from its by-products. It is used to make a special kind of coke (coke is the residue of a distilling process which turns coal into a gray, carbon-rich, reliable fuel). And the carbon recovered from anthracite lines pots and molds in the making of steel. Anthracite is used to make "charcoal" briquets (for outdoor cooking), and to burn cement and lime. Much of it is burned to cure tobacco, and for use in greenhouses and hatcheries—wherever a clean, steady heat is needed.

The carbon in anthracite is used in telephones and in making battery cases and other pieces of electronic equipment. The ash that remains after anthracite has been burned is an excellent conditioner for soils and is also used in manufacturing building blocks.

Anthracite, the king of coals, lies deeper in the earth than does bituminous coal. Nearly all the anthracite in the United States lies beneath the ground in five counties in northeastern Pennsylvania. (However, sometimes, where anthracite is found, bituminous coal is also found—and vice versa.) Small beds of hard coal are also found in Alaska, Arkansas, Colorado, New Mexico, Washington, and Virginia. Approximately 6 billion tons of it have been mined, leaving an estimated reserve that is enough to last for two or three centuries, depending upon how fast it will be used.

The annual peak production of anthracite reached 100 million tons in 1917. Since then other forms of energy have competed with it to such a degree that only 20 million tons are now mined each year. This decline has caused severe social and economic depressions in the hard-coal areas.

The other anthracite-producing countries of the world are in much the same condition, producing less and less hard coal because of the competition of other fuel sources. Their reserves are regarded as national secrets, but those in the Soviet Union, Great Britain, and Germany might match our own.

However, because of the energy crisis, our use of anthracite will probably change. The Bureau of Mines, in cooperation with the mining industry, is seeking to improve the methods of mining hard coal and of preparing and making more use of it. And so, if it can be dug at smaller expense and new uses are found for it, the tonnage of anthracite will probably be more than was produced in the early years of the twentieth century.

### BITUMINOUS COAL

When coal is mentioned in modern times, it is usually bituminous coal that is meant. There is more of it than of anthracite, and it can be used for many more purposes than any other type of coal. Bituminous coal is found in many places in the United States, but the largest beds are in the Appalachian area, located in a section stretching from Ohio and Pennsylvania into Alabama.

At the beginning of this century, more than 3,000 bituminous mines were in operation, employing 300,000 workers. Production was 215 million tons annually. In 1918, when soft coal contributed 75 percent of our nation's energy, 580 million tons were taken from the earth. By 1923 there were 9,000 mines, employing 700,000 people. There was a lull in the operation of the mines during the depression of the thirties, when production fell. More than 3,000 mines closed, and the number of employees dropped to 300,000.

However, in the years following World War II, when the devastated countries of Europe were struggling to rehabilitate their economic systems, production increased to 630 million tons annually. Nevertheless, although the mining of bituminous coal climbed rapidly, its total share of the world's energy market declined, because of the increased production of natural gas and petroleum.

The giant locomotives that pulled people and material across the country, with firemen shoveling black stones into the red mouths of fireboxes, were no more. The huge ships that plowed through the seas no longer needed bunkers filled with coal to drive their engines. Trains and ships used the new magic fuel—oil.

But still the production of bituminous coal increased! Though some of its largest users were turning to other means of energy, still other consumers continued to demand more and more soft coal.

Tremendous amounts are used by the steel industry in manufacturing coke for their ovens and hearths. And the country's increasing demand for more electricity has forced the public utilities to consume a great deal of coal to make steam to drive their generators. Atomic power is being used in many areas for that purpose, but it has created problems and raised opposition among people anxious over the possibility of nuclear accidents. Therefore the demand for bituminous coal is expected to grow, and it is estimated that by the 1990's it will have to be mined at the fantastic rate of 800 million tons annually, three times the amount being consumed now.

The reserves of our bituminous coal beds are enormous, however. The Bureau of Mines claims that this nation contains one third of the known bituminous-coal deposits in the world. A federal geological survey estimated, in January 1960, that at least 1,660 billion tons in this country could be mined by conventional methods, and the coal that could be mined from difficult places—under the seas and from great depths in the earth—might be *eight times* more. With the technological improvements that are certain to come, most of these previously "inaccessible" beds will be mined too.

## Lignite

Lignite is a very soft fuel, one of the many stages of coal development between peat and bituminous coal. In this country the largest deposits of lignite are in Texas, Montana, and both North and South Dakota. It has a brownish-black color, and for that reason is often called brown coal.

Brown coal is used as a domestic fuel and also to generate electric power, but only in the localities where it is produced. It is less expensive than anthracite or bituminous coal, but it doesn't burn as well. However, in the past few years, we have begun to use more and more lignite as a source of carbon, which is easily recovered from it.

Another increasing use of lignite is in the manufacture of gases. The Department of the Interior, through the Bureau of Mines, has been experimenting with a special gas that can be used in the production of ammonia, synthetic liquid fuels, and chemicals.

## Cannel and Boghead Coal

Another of the various coallike fuels is cannel coal. The English gave it the name. To the early Britons the flame of this grayish, velvety coal looked like the flame of a burning candle, so they called it candle coal, which over the centuries became "cannel coal."

Methane and coke can be made from cannel coal. It

burns like wood and has heated European homes for hundreds of years. Many Americans, too, have discovered that cannel coal is a delight to burn in their fireplaces. It burns slowly and steadily and gives off very little smoke.

Geologists believe that cannel coal was made in the very stagnant waters of the forests that finally became the hard coals. Very often cannel-coal deposits are in or around oil shales, and petroleum is easily recovered from it. In some beds in Arkansas, thirty gallons of oil can be recovered from one ton of cannel coal. But there isn't enough of it to make large-scale recovery possible.

Boghead coal is also found in small amounts near or in the beds of other coals. It differs from cannel coal in that it is tough and elastic. Geologists believe that boghead coal was formed by jellylike masses of material that sank to the bottoms of swamps. Its chief use is in making coal tar—almost half of each ton can be made into tar. It was discovered around 1850 near the town of Boghead in Scotland, and so acquired its name. Like cannel coal, it would be a very profitable fuel if more were available.

## PEAT

Peat is the partially decomposed plant matter that has accumulated under water and in swamps. It is the first stage of the coal-making process, before pressure has been applied to it over millions of years.

Nature is still making peat in many parts of the world, and more of it is being used now than ever before, not only for heating houses in areas where it is found, but for other important purposes.

Peat is one of the oldest fuels known to man. When the Romans conquered northern and western Europe, they recorded that the natives "burned earth" to keep warm. They were astonished to see the inhabitants of these regions tear up pieces of sod, dry it, and then burn it in fireplaces.

Within the past few years peat has even been used as an industrial fuel in some countries, and this use has increased. The Soviet Union and Ireland burn huge quantities of peat to generate electric power. In the past the United States did use peat for commercial fuel, but only until the development of better means of transportation could bring enough coal to industrial centers.

There are large deposits of peat in at least thirty-five states, with total reserves estimated at 14 billion tons. Florida, Michigan, Minnesota, and Wisconsin have the largest deposits. More than half of the peat in the United States is in Minnesota, where deposits at least five feet thick contain approximately 7 billion tons. Florida has 2 million tons, most of it in the Everglades.

Although large amounts of peat are used in the United States, only a small part is employed as fuel. It is an excellent soil improver, and gardeners use millions of bales of the spongy material every year. The use of peat in gardens in the United States has doubled in the past ten years.

Researchers, especially in European countries, are trying to find more uses for peat. In addition to developing it as a fuel for electric power, they are trying to find ways of recovering gas and chemicals from it. The Soviet Union has laboratories and experimental stations solely for the development of peat. They even have colleges that train technicians in the use of the material. The Moscow Peat Institute, established in 1930, graduates between two hundred and three hundred scientists yearly, all to be involved in research programs for the better use of peat. Ireland, too, has experimental stations and scientists who are devoted to finding more ways to use that country's major source of fuel.

In the United States peat can't compete as a fuel, but as the population increases, there will be more and more demand for this wonderful soil improver, which helps the earth produce more and better crops.

And so the word "coal" includes a variety of fossil

fuels. All are similar in that they are a legacy of energy left to us from an ancient past, but all of them differ in the ways they can be used.

How these deposits of energy are taken from the earth, and how they are prepared so that their many mysteries can benefit us as well as future generations, is the next chapter in the story of coal.

# 4 Mining the Different Kinds of Coal

UNDERGROUND MINING TECHNIQUES

In 1805, this advertisement appeared in the *Federalist,* a newspaper published in Wilkes-Barre, Pennsylvania:

> The Subscriber takes this method of informing the public that he understands the miner's work. He worked for twenty-three years in the mines of Wales, one year and a half in Schuyler's copper mines in New Jersey, and three years in Ogden's mine in the same State. If anyone thinks there is any ore in his lands, he understands it, wet or dry. He will work by the day or by the solid foot or yard, at reasonable wages or for country produce.

Today, of course, miners don't need to advertise for employment. And an offer to pay them in "country produce" would be a quick way to bring on a strike. But that advertisement, when compared to the hundreds of thousands of people who are employed in the mining industry today, shows how amazingly that industry has grown in approximately 170 years.

Coal miners wait in a steel-roofed "mantrip car" to descend a long, sloping tunnel to the level of the coal seam.

*Monterey Coal Company*

To tear from the ground all the types and quantities of coal that are needed to satisfy our country's demand for more and ever more energy requires all kinds of mining.

Mining coal, to most people, means shafts descending miles down into the bowels of the earth, and elevators crowded with dirty-faced men who wear lights on their caps. Mining, to many, also means disasters, with men trapped in tunnels to die slowly of suffocation, or be quickly killed by the explosions of coal dust and gases. News pictures show groups of stoic women waiting at mine entrances for news of husbands, sons, and brothers, whose lives are being extinguished in caves beneath the earth.

Most anthracite and bituminous coal is still cut from veins of black rock deep underground. Men still ride up and down in elevators to and from tunnels that spread like the streets of a vast underground city.

But now the faces of the miners are not always streaked with black. Often they are a ghostly white. For to avoid (as much as possible) the dangers of explosions, the coal veins and the tunnel walls are sprayed with a solution of finely crushed limestone.

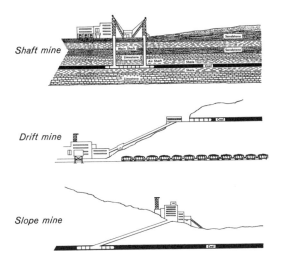

In a shaft mine the miners are taken to the coal seam by elevators, and the coal is removed to the surface by the same method. In a drift mine the entrance is vertical into a hillside. In a slope mine the entrance slants downward to the seam.

*National Coal Association*

Underground mining is much safer now than it was in the past, but, according to insurance companies, it is still the country's most hazardous occupation. More than 1,000 American miners die every year because of explosions, fires, sudden floods, the collapsing of the ceilings of worked-out areas, and particularly of "black lung"—a disease caused by years of breathing coal dust.

There are three principal ways to mine coal from deep veins: shaft, slope, and drift mining. In *shaft mining,* vertical shafts are dug directly downward to meet a vein of coal. As the coal is broken from the vein and sent to the surface, the tunnel is extended deeper or widened horizontally, to follow the ribbon of coal.

*Drift mining* is done when a vein lies along the side of a hill, and a shaft is dug directly into the coal. The

Above: Loading coal into a car (see background) that will travel on
rails to a central station in the mine.

*United Mine Workers of America*

Below: Miners with the dogs that were sometimes used to pull the
coal-filled carts.                    *United Mine Workers of America*

Miner using a pickax.
*National Coal Association*

Mine mules and child workers.                    *Library of Congress*

tunnel is extended horizontally along the side of the hill as the vein is excavated.

A *slope mine* is a tunnel dug at an angle to meet a vein that does not lie close enough to the surface for strip mining. The tunnel then follows the vein vertically or horizontally.

For many years the actual mining was done in the same way. Coal was chopped or cut from the face of the vein by picks, then shoveled into small cars that ran on rails and were pushed by men or dragged by animals to a central station, where elevators carried the rough coal to the surface.

## MEN AND MULES

Many stories were told about the mules that dragged the cars. It was said that the animals never saw the surface of the earth, that they were born and spent their lives deep in the mines, and that a new breed of mules had come into existence—blind animals that needed no eyes.

This is totally untrue. The mine mules were valuable animals. In many cases the mine owners treated them better than they did the men who toiled in the same tunnels. The mules worked in shifts, were fed well, and allowed on the surface for longer periods than they spent underground. The mules were an investment to be cared for. The better they were treated, the longer they could be expected to work, and the more years they worked, the better would be the owner's return on his original investment.

The men and boys who worked in the deep tunnels were not so fortunate. Human beings were expected to take care of themselves, and they were expendable. When some of them died because of poor food, overwork, or age, other workers were eager to step into their places.

Those early miners were paid as little as possible— only enough so they could buy food (at high prices) from

Breaker boys at work. *The Smithsonian Institution*

the company store, run by the mine owners, and to pay rent for the hovels they lived in, also owned by the mine operators.

Anthracite and bituminous coal contain varying amounts of impurities when they come from the mines. Slate and bits of wood are some of the most common materials that must be removed before coal can be sent to consumers. The main function of a preparation plant for coal is to break the large pieces into smaller ones, remove the impurities, and separate the coal into various sizes.

Those early preparation plants, or "breakers," were one of the main reasons why unions were formed, and were one of the reasons for many years of violence in the coalfields. They were cruel and dangerous places in which to work. Small boys (some as young as five years of age), called breaker boys, sat astride wooden chutes down which the raw coal flowed like black streams. Their job was to pick out the impurities and sort the coal into different sizes as it passed.

It was hard labor. The hands of a breaker boy, after only a few weeks, looked like the claws of a blackbird. Many of the boys were so small they were carried to the breakers in the early dawn on the shoulders of their fathers, who then went into the tunnels to do their day's labor of fourteen hours.

When the boys were twelve years old, they graduated to swinging a pick or shoveling in the mines. Some small boys were sent directly into the deep shafts, because some of the tunnels were so narrow that only little boys could work in them.

Child-labor laws were passed, prohibiting boys from working in the mines until they were twelve, but the laws were ignored or not enforced. It was only when mechanized equipment was able to do the menial jobs better and cheaper that the day of the breaker boys passed into history.

## Modern Methods

Now, after years of strife, unions have obtained better safety laws and higher pay for those who work in the mines. Today 99 percent of all coal is mechanically mined. Fewer men are employed than in the past, yet more tons of coal are taken from the earth.

A variety of complex machines is used in mining today. Some of them cut, load, and transport the coal in one continuous operation. Other machines, called mobile cutters, cut under, above, and along the sides of a vein. Then, after blastings have torn the coal loose, loading machines scoop up the pieces and dump them on

A miner inserts a compressed-air cartridge into a hole drilled in the face of a coal seam. Air compressed to 10,000 pounds per square inch will be valved into the cartridge through flexible tubing at its rear. The pressure builds up until it ruptures a plastic seal and bursts out with explosive force, breaking up the coal for loading.

*National Coal Association*

The operator of a continuous mining machine at Monterey Coal Company's No. 1 mine at Carlinville, Illinois, sits under a protective canopy mounted on his machine. On his chest he wears a device that samples the coal dust in the air he breathes. Tubing in the background aids mine ventilation.

*National Coal Association*

Exhibiting more teeth than a shark, the ripper head of a continuous mining machine moves up to a coal seam. These machines rip coal from the seams with steel bits, scoop it up, and load it into shuttle cars or conveyor belts, thus eliminating the conventional steps of undercutting, drilling, blasting, and loading the coal.

*National Coal Association*

conveyor belts, which carry them to shuttle cars, and these cars are then pulled to the surface, not by mules, but by small engines.

The most widely used machines, each run by one man, tear coal from the face of a vein with spinning steel teeth. Each machine can do in a day the amount of work it required a dozen men to do in the same time in the past.

A continuous mining machine especially designed for low coal seams digs out and loads coal at the rate of four tons a minute. The rotary cutting heads and trimming chain pivot until they almost meet at the center. The lower part of the chain carries the loosened coal back to the built-in conveyor which loads it into the shuttle cars to begin the trip out of the mine.

*Joy Manufacturing Company*

The counter-rotating arms of a continuous mining machine rip an arched tunnel through seams of bituminous coal. Such machines can dig up to eight tons of coal per minute.

*Joy Manufacturing Company*

"Longwall mining" is when a specially built machine moves horizontally beside a seam, ripping away the coal as it goes. Here a miner operates his longwall machine under the protection of movable steel roof supports. Whirling cutters move back and forth over the face, slicing off the coal. It falls onto a conveyor below the machine and is moved to the haulage-way. The movable roof props are advanced as the miner works farther along the coal seam and the roof behind is permitted to fall.

*Eastern Associated Coal Corporation*

These machines creep forward, leaving behind "rooms" cut from the vein. The ceilings of these rooms are supported by pillars of coal, props of wood, or metal roof bolts. Roof bolts are relatively new in mining. As the machines move ahead, holes are bored into the roofs of the tunnels, then long expansion bolts are inserted and tightened, to bind the overlying rocks to the tunnel ceilings.

As the mining of coal became more mechanized, so did the sorting and cleaning of it.

Before being cleaned, the coal, taken directly from the mine, is sent to the "tipple," a building that performs the work that used to be done by the breaker boys. In the tipple the coat is sorted into various sizes—egg, stove, nut, pea—by being pushed across a series of screens.

Two different methods of cleaning coal are now being used: *froth flotation,* and the *heavy-medium cyclone process.*

In the froth-flotation method, coal is fed into a chemical bath, and air is forced through the solution. Pieces of coal are attracted to the froth of bubbles and rise to the

Loading machine with crablike arms moves through mine to where it will sweep lumps of coal onto its central conveyor, which will drop them onto a shuttle car to begin the trip out of the mine. Steel canopy protects operator from roof falls, and flourescent lights along sides of the machine illuminate the working area, supplementing the machine's headlights and the miner's cap lamp.

*Consolidation Coal Company*

top to be removed. The impurities fall to the bottom of the tank.

When the heavy-medium cyclone process is used, coal is put into water that contains magnetite, a type of iron ore that is naturally magnetic (this ore is sometimes called *lodestone,* because of its magnetic qualities). The liquid is then forced into cones that whirl at fantastic speeds. The magnetism of the magnetite attracts trace minerals and other impurities, which are forced out of the narrow ends of the cones, while the cleaned coal is pushed out of the wide parts of the cones. The magnetite is not recovered. It is considered a necessary expense of this operation.

### Strip Mining

When coal lies close to the surface of the earth, it is recovered by strip mining or the open-pit method. More coal is produced each year by these two procedures than by deep mining. The invention of mechanical shovels, excavators, and scrapers has made strip and pit methods much cheaper than recovering coal from mines deep in the earth.

In strip mining, the surface of the earth that covers the vein is removed—or stripped away—laying bare the coal, which is then broken or blasted by huge pneumatic drills and hauled to the preparation plants in trucks. There is no need for shafts or tunnels, or expensive

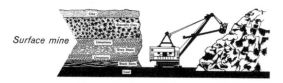

In a surface mine giant excavating equipment removes layers of rock and earth from over the coal, which is then removed by smaller shovels.          *National Coal Association*

A surface mining shovel, tall as a twenty-story building, takes a 140-cubic-yard bite of earth and rock—about 210 tons—in a coal mine near Marissa, Illinois. It can turn, dump this load more than a city block away, and return for another bite in less than a minute. The machine digs no coal—it exposes the seam, shown here beneath its eight-foot-high crawler treads, so that smaller shovels can load the coal into trucks. The automobile near the treads shows the size of the machine. *Bucyrus-Erie Coal Company*

equipment such as elevators or conveyor systems. The coal is mined on the surface of the land. Where a vein is very thick, a pit might be dug to recover all the coal, but it remains open to the sky.

Usually in strip mining the earth cover is removed by power shovels, the way the foundation of a house is excavated. In the early days this left the countryside

A gigantic walking dragline—the world's largest at the time of its construction—dumps 85 cubic yards of earth and rock that it has scooped off a coal seam at the Homestead Mine of the Peabody Coal Company in western Kentucky. The boom of this machine is 275 feet long. The machine revolves on a large circular base. It moves from place to place by lifting itself on the long "shoes" beside the base, like a man walking on crutches.

*Bucyrus-Erie Coal Company*

hideously scarred. Beautiful fields were pockmarked with open pits where stagnant water settled. What had once been green land became bare clay and loose dirt. Abandoned strip mines were offensive to see and unpleasant to live near.

Finally the actions of the strip-mine operators became so careless that states passed laws to control them, to make certain that the surface of the land was left as beautiful as it was before their giant shovels bit into it.

Now, before strip mining can begin in an area, the operators must supply the mining department of that

The dipper of a surface coal mining shovel dwarfs a mechanic, left, as it lifts 140 cubic yards—about 210 tons—of earth and rock. Once every minute the shovel removes this much overburden, about three railroad carloads, from above a coal seam near Marissa, Illinois. Smaller shovels load the coal into trucks.

*Bucyrus-Erie Coal Company*

The world's largest truck is this off-highway giant that carries a 240-ton load from the pit of a surface mine to a preparation plant nearby. The truck has power units front and rear, and can be driven from either end, so that it can reverse its direction of travel without turning around, or it can use both units and travel sideways. It serves the Captain Mine of Southwestern Illinois Coal Corporation.

*National Coal Association*

The fish are really biting at this lake that is part of a sprawling 100,000-acre strip coal mine owned and operated by the Ohio Power Company. Whenever possible—after removing the coal—Ohio Power converts its mined land into lakes. There are more than 350 on this mine site in Morgan, Muskingum, and Noble counties. Thousands of other lakes throughout the United States have been made by responsible coal companies reclaiming their mined land.
*Columbus, Ohio,* Daily News

state with detailed maps showing exactly where the mining is to be done, and also how they intend to prevent water from entering pits and how they will "backfill" the scars on the land after they have removed the coal. "Backfilling" means that the pits will be filled in and covered with rich topsoil and grass and trees planted. In many modern strip-mining operations, the topsoil that covers the vein of coal is carefully cut and peeled away, then replaced after the coal has been taken.

Many mining communities owe their parks and recreational areas to the planning of strip-mining operators, who have carefully replaced the disturbed earth, sometimes making the land more beautiful than it was before. Sometimes forests have been planted on land that has been scarred by strip mining. Many millions of pine seedlings have been planted on mined-out areas in Pennsylvania. The trees have been so successful that the Pennsylvania Coal Industry boasts the slogan "Coal for Today—Timber for Tomorrow."

Sometimes a vein of coal turns down into the earth in strip mining. Then a special type of machine is used to follow it for long distances. It performs the way a brace drill does when boring into wood. But instead of wood shavings spiraling out, these bits, or augers, bring coal

Auger mining is useful in hilly areas where coal seams continue under rising land too thick for economical surface mining. The auger twists into the seam like a carpenter's bit, drawing out the coal to a conveyor that loads it into trucks. These West Virginia miners are inserting a twenty-six-foot auger section into a string of augers already in operation in the coal seam.

*U.S. Bureau of Mines*

to the surface. The holes they bore into the earth are from 16 to 52 inches in diameter, and the coal drilled out is loaded into trucks and hauled away.

Because each auger is operated by only one man, the method is very economical. The machine can average 39 tons a day, as compared to 29 tons for an ordinary strip-mining machine and 13 tons per day for machinery used in deep mining.

## MINING ANTHRACITE

Anthracite, the glamour product of the mining industry, burns longer, with less smoke, and gives a more intense heat than other coals. However, because it usually lies deeper in the earth, it is more difficult to mine. It costs more per ton, and so less of it is used.

In the early days of anthracite mining, much of the waste material (very fine pieces of the coal) were piled beside the breakers and regarded as useless. One of the most depressing sights in the anthracite regions of northeastern Pennsylvania are the huge mountains of fine, almost powdered coal that lie beside abandoned mines and breakers.

But with the invention of furnaces that can economically burn coal as fine as powder, these black mountains are almost worth their weight in money. This former waste material is washed and then delivered to power companies, which burn it to generate electricity.

Another welcome recovery for anthracite mine operators is the immense amount of fine coal being reclaimed from riverbeds. In the past, when coal was cleaned, much of the waste was washed into rivers and creeks. The three large rivers in the anthracite region of eastern Pennsylvania—the Lehigh, Schuylkill, and Susquehanna—have on their bottoms a thick layer of very fine coal, known as anthrafine. Only dredges are necessary to recover a product of great value.

## DANGERS OF SHAFT MINES

Even though now there are more and better safety rules, mining is still one of the most dangerous of all occupations. And the greatest hazard is explosion. Gases of many kinds are always present in mines. In the past, caged birds, usually canaries, were placed in deep shafts and tunnels. If only a small amount of gas was in the area, the birds would become agitated and often die. This warning would give the miners time to escape from that particular shaft or tunnel. Now complex electronic equipment is used for the same purpose. But even this warning system isn't perfect. Gases and coal dust still accumulate, and and if there is a spark from a falling rock, the result may be an explosion.

Some of the most dangerous places for explosions are in the "rooms" left behind as the cutting machines creep forward. Even though the roofs are propped by wood or even roof bolts, there are always cracks that are made by pressure. Gases can escape into the rooms, and when there is an accidental spark, the result is disaster.

Sometimes, too, props left behind to hold up the roofs of tunnels will collapse because of age or neglect. Then miners are often buried alive, or their way to the surface is barred by tons of rock and coal.

Another danger is caused by "run-of-the-mill" coal. "Run-of-the-mill" is powdered coal plus bits and pieces that fall from the underground cars and are swept into piles. If left too long unremoved, as happens in badly run mines, these "scrap heaps" of coal release gases that can be exploded by the smallest spark. Sometimes an explosion can even be set off by chemical action, which is generated by heat inside the piles themselves.

Water is always present to some degree in underground mining and is usually kept under control. But once in a while the strata, or rock layers, which protect the tunnels from an underground river, will be too thin or weakened by explosions. Then the stream will break through the walls of floors and maroon or drown the men working in that tunnel. Also, surface floods, caused by heavy rains, sometimes pour into mine openings, trapping miners underground.

Deep-pit mining can never be completely safe. Working deep in the earth, man is fighting against forces that are far stronger than he is.

### MINING LIGNITE AND "WINNING" PEAT

The mining of brown coal, or lignite, is similar to the recovery of bituminous coal. Most lignite lies close to the surface and is mined by the strip method.

Beds of lignite vary in thickness from approximately 3 to 25 feet or more. The preparation of lignite for market is not as difficult as the preparation of bituminous coal or anthracite. Usually only one grade of lignite is used, and that is from the center of the vein. In this way many impurities are eliminated that require additional processing with other types of coal. After mining, the lignite is crushed and treated with an oil spray to reduce dust. It is then sent to special furnaces that can burn it economically. Lignite contains more moisture than other coals, and therefore it produces only half the heat of bituminous coal or anthracite.

Peat, as mentioned earlier, is the partly decomposed plant material that forms the basic material of coal beds. The odor of burning peat can never be forgotten. In many of the villages of Ireland, Wales, and other parts of Europe, the aroma of peat lies like a sweet perfume over the countryside.

Mining peat has been called "winning" peat for as long as there have been cottages in which to burn it. The term is passing away now, but in some countries, especially Ireland, the expression is still widely used.

To "win" peat from a bog is very much like slicing a flat cake. The peat lies on top of the ground and can easily be stripped away in pieces, usually three or four feet long and three to five inches thick. If the bed is thicker, layer after layer can be removed until the earth is exposed.

The strips of peat are usually quite wet and must be spread in the open air to dry. When peat is dried in the open, it usually takes about six weeks before it is ready to be burned in a fireplace.

In the United States (as in all countries where large quantities of peat are used commercially) it is mined by machines, then stacked on racks and dried artificially.

Mining peat by machine varies according to the location of the bogs, the type of the material, and what it is to be used for. But most of it is done by loosening the surface of the bog with huge disc harrows. Afterward bulldozers push the layers to where trucks haul it to the drying plants. If the bog is extremely wet, it is partially dried by means of drainage ditches and pumping.

There are several varieties of peat gathered in the United States. In Michigan, long lasting reed-sedge peat is mined by the harrow-and-bulldozer method, and in Indiana moss peat is gathered by dragging huge scrapers across the surface of the bog. In Minnesota peat is harvested by vacuum; after the material has been loosened by harrows, machines move across the bog and lift the peat by air suction, like giant vacuum cleaners, then carry it to the waiting trucks.

## TRANSPORTING COAL

The increasing need for coal in private houses and the country's young industries was a principal reason for the development of our vast modern transportation systems.

Canals came first. It was soon discovered that floating long barges on water was considerably easier than pulling wagons over rutted roads. But most inland rivers were navigable only in frequently interrupted stretches, until rapids or waterfalls or shallows made travel impossible even by canoe. So canals were dug, usually alongside the rivers they were to replace. They averaged three to ten feet deep and twenty feet wide. Movable barriers, called sluice gates, regulated the flow of river water in and out of the canals. Most of them were privately owned, and tolls were paid at various places along the routes, the way tolls are collected today on many of our highways.

Where it was possible, the canal boats or barges were loaded at mine entrances, then pulled by horses, mules, and sometimes men to most of the towns along the eastern seacoast. When the coal was unloaded, the barges were cleaned, then piled high with vegetables and other merchandise, and pulled back over the canals again.

Railroads were able to speed the transportation of coal. As the iron-and-steel rails spread across the land and larger and more powerful engines dragged longer and longer lines of cars, the slower canal boats passed into history.

In many parts of the country, canals can still be seen alongside rivers. Most have dried up or are filled with stagnant water, and grass covers the paths that once were trod by straining men and animals, pulling barges carrying food and fuel to families in distant towns.

Meanwhile the immense coal industry of today and its powerful union were coming into being through years of struggle and turbulence. None of those years were as violent as those when the Molly McGuires ruled eastern Pennsylvania.

# **5** The Molly McGuires

COAL-COUNTRY TERRORISM

Early on a sunny spring morning in 1866, on a country road on the outskirts of Pottsville, Pennsylvania, a man was walking queerly. His face was bloody, and the black hole of his mouth gulped the nippy air. His tongue had been cut out. His arms hung strangely from his shoulders. Both had been broken in several places.

A few days later in Tamaqua, a town in the same coal-producing area, a man answered a knock on his door. When he opened it, three men shot him dead. The men didn't run. They didn't hurry. They strolled away casually.

Both these men were the owners of mines in that section of Pennsylvania. Their murders were only two of the hundreds of violent deaths among mine officials between 1862 and 1876. For more than twenty-five years, five eastern counties of Pennsylvania were without law or order. All this was caused by a band of Irish miners who called themselves the Molly McGuires, or the Mollies.

Lower Fifth Avenue at the Southwestern Mine in Colorado. Note the company-owned shacks the miners lived in.

*United Mine Workers of America*

Almost every man in Schuylkill, Carbon, Luzerne, Lehigh, and Lackawanna counties was directly or indirectly connected with the digging of anthracite coal. Even the few police had relatives who daily went deep into the mines. These men wouldn't inform on a brother, neighbor, or fellow worker, because the penalty of informing was swift death or torture. Far better to see nothing, to know nothing.

Why?

### OPPRESSION

In 1860 the average pay of a miner was ten cents an hour. Because of layoffs and "penalties" for minor infractions, his eighty hours of work per week earned him an average of four dollars. That was on the better weeks—it was less most of the year, and he was expected to support a family of four, five, or six on those few dollars. He also lived in a shack, one of long lines of shanties that were built by the owners close to their mines. They were called shantytowns.

Even the four dollars a week didn't really belong to the miner. Some of it was deducted each week for rent for his "home." And the only store in each shantytown was the company store, or "pluck me," as the miners called it. These stores were owned and operated by the mine owners, and prices were often more than 25 percent higher than in other stores in the surrounding communities.

The miner *had* to buy his supplies in these stores. If he didn't, his name was handed to his foreman, and he was fired. His name was put on a blacklist, and no other mine owner would hire him.

The company store gave credit—not only gave it, but insisted on it. Its purpose was to get the miner in debt as soon as possible. From then on he was a slave. Each week, although his debt was deducted from the pay, the sum he owed grew larger. The miner couldn't quit, couldn't take his family to another part of the country. Even if he had enough courage to move, he had no cash. Everything the family needed—even funerals—was supplied by the store. The miner was chained to the store and to the mine. And as his children grew, they, too, worked in the mines, and *their* pay was applied to the debt of the father and sometimes as payment on debts of *his* father.

A New York newspaper in an editorial dated April 10, 1872, described the plight of a hard-coal miner: "Sometimes generation after generation works to pay back debts begun by their grandfathers. Those who have a few coins in their pockets earn them by menial labor after working long hours in the earth."

The life of a miner's children was harsh and cruel. At

Kitchen in miner's house.         *U.S. Bureau of Mines*

Miner's daughter washing clothes in company-owned house (1946).
        *U.S. Bureau of Mines*

the age of five or six young lads were taken to the breakers to sort coal with their fingers for days that lasted fourteen weary hours. There were no schools. Children born in the coal regions grew to manhood and womanhood not knowing how to write their names. When the boys became twelve years old, they entered the mines to labor beside their fathers and grandfathers. In time they, too, had families and became slaves of the mines.

### THE IRISH ARRIVE

How did this begin? Why did men allow themselves to become captives in the mines of eastern Pennsylvania?

There were three reasons. First, it was the beginning of the Industrial Revolution. New factories were being started and old ones were expanding, and so more coal was needed to supply the energy they required. Second, the average American refused to go into the mines to dig coal, at the risk of his life and for little pay. Third, something happened in Ireland, three thousand miles away from the mines—a potato famine.

For many generations the Irish people had depended on their potato crops. They exported them. They were the most important part of their diet—indeed, many poor Irish families ate nothing else. Irish life depended on potatoes.

Then, in the years 1845, 1846, and 1847, a disease struck the potato fields, and the crops failed. Irish people starved by the thousands. More thousands of them left their homeland to find work and food in other parts of the world. During the next five years almost *two million* of them came to the United States.

They didn't make that decision alone. The mine owners of the United States sent salesmen to Ireland to sell the "dream" of America. There would be high wages, lovely houses, schools for their children, and many opportunities in the land far across the sea, where everyone was equal.

The dream became a nightmare. Most of the Irishmen who signed up for the free passage to America were uneducated farmers. When they arrived in America, they and their families were herded into trains and sent directly to the mines.

The high wages were ten cents an hour. The lovely houses were shanties. There were no schools. The "opportunities" were jobs deep in the mines, where tunnels collapsed, gases exploded, and safety rules were unknown.

The Irish miners were defenseless. They were in a foreign land, without friends or money. There were no welfare agencies, no unions. In some parts of the coalfields, a few miners began to form groups that attempled to talk with the owners and tried to ease some of the intolerable working conditions. But these first unions were weak, and the answer of the mine owners was to import more Irishmen. When there were two or three men for every job, the father of a family hesitated before making complaints.

### SECRET SOCIETY

And so the Molly McGuires were formed. There are many legends about their name. But the true one seems to be that they called themselves after an Irish widow, Molly McGuire, who was put into the street by her English landlord and forced to beg for food for her children.

Not all the Irishmen who worked in the mines were Molly McGuires—but all the Mollies were Irish. They were a secret group who were dedicated to the belief that the only way to obtain fair treatment from the mine owners was to terrorize them.

In the early years of the violence almost all the miners were proud of their countrymen's exploits. When a mine boss was beaten, or a bomb blew up and ruined a mine, they felt some pride.

But as the Mollies killed and maimed more mine

officials, and more property was destroyed by burnings and explosions, the average miner was appalled. But no one did anything to stop the terror, for the deepest hatred of the Mollies was reserved for an informer. Any miner who spoke against the Mollies or gave information about them, to obtain a better shanty or a little more pay, could expect swift and terrible revenge.

Finally the crimes of the Mollies became so open and so many that the mine owners banded together to stop this gang of murderers, who had terrorized the coal counties for so long.

There were plenty of miners in the area, for salesmen were still in Ireland selling the "dream" of America. But now there was a scarcity of bosses and operators. Not many men wanted those jobs, for the life of an operator or a superintendent wasn't very safe. Each year more than half of them were killed or beaten so badly they were unable to work. Production of coal began to decline, and that hurt profits. Something had to be done.

The mine owners elected Franklin Benjamin Gowan, a fellow mine operator, and gave him complete authority to do anything possible to stop the activities of the Mollies. Gowan realized that the only way to bring the Mollies to justice was to know—and be able to prove—the names of the leaders of the gang and the crimes they had done. The only way to do that was to place an informer inside the group. But that seemed to be impossible. For the spy would have to be a very special man. He would have to be Irish and know how to work in the mines. Somehow he would have to wangle his way into membership in the Mollies, and he would need enough courage to die if he was discovered. There was only one place where a man like that might be found—the Pinkerton National Detective Agency in Chicago.

Major Allan Pinkerton, a Scotsman, had been a member of the Chicago Police Department and in time became its chief. Soon afterward he started his own detective agency, which became so famous it was known as "the eye that never sleeps." He was also responsible for the creation of the United States' Secret Service. If anyone could help the mine owners, Pinkerton was that man.

At a meeting in Chicago, Gowan outlined the problem to Pinkerton. "The man we need will have to be one of the greatest actors who ever spoke a line," he told the detective. "For if he gives a poor performance, he'll be dead."

Pinkerton promised to try to find a man for the job, and a week later he and Gowan had another meeting. The detective said: "When I push this button and that door opens, you'll see the only man I know who can do the job you want done." He pressed the button.

In the doorway stood a grinning, redheaded, blue-eyed Irishman.

"This is James McParlan," Pinkerton said. "He *wants* to do the job."

### Infiltrating the Mollies

McParlan had been born in Ulster, Ireland, twenty-eight years before. He was a small man—five feet seven inches tall—and weighed only 145 pounds. But those pounds were all muscle. He'd been a professional boxer and a deckhand on ships, and had herded sheep in Australia. He loved danger and excitement. That was why he had become a detective and why he accepted the job Gowan offered. But there was another reason, too.

"I'm Irish," he said, "and I've heard of the Mollies. They make a real Irishman ashamed. I'll do everything I can to stop them."

That was the beginning of the end of the Molly McGuires.

Late in the autumn of 1873 a small Irishman, red-headed, blue-eyed, and dressed in the scuffed and soiled clothing of a miner, strolled into a saloon in a small town in Schuylkill County, in eastern Pennsylvania, and ordered a drink. The man was James McParlan, but he'd changed his name to James McKenna.

From that moment his life was in danger every minute of every hour. He had a friendly personality and went from saloon to saloon in many towns in the coal regions, buying drinks and talking. He explained he'd won some money in Philadelphia and wouldn't go back to work until he'd spent all of it.

Finally McParlan (now McKenna) rented a room in Tamaqua, one of the coal towns, where he had a feeling the leaders of the Mollies had their headquarters. He soon got a job in one of the mines and began to mix with the other miners.

Slowly McParlan began to be accepted in the town. And even more slowly he came to know some of the members of the Molly McGuires. He bought them drinks, joked with them, and even held his own in some saloon brawls. He became known as a devil-may-care little man who loved to take chances.

At last one night he was taken to meet Jack Kehoe who, he had discovered, was the leader of the Mollies. Kehoe liked the carefree little Irishman and gradually let him into the secrets of the secret society. At a ceremony one night in Kehoe's shanty, in which he signed his name with his own blood, McParlan was officially made a Son of Molly McGuire.

It took four more years. But in the end McParlan completed, bit by bit, the testimony he was to give in a courtroom in the town of Mauch Chunk, (now Jim Thorpe) seat of Carbon County—testimony that sent Jack Kehoe and other Mollies to their deaths by hanging.

On the stand McParlan, in a steady voice, read his report, in which were written names and dates, and all the conversations of the meetings he had attended when the Molly McGuires planned killings, beatings, and dynamitings.

On a summer morning in 1877 two Irishmen, dressed in new black suits and each carrying a red rose in his callused hands, walked to a gallows in the prison yard at Pottsville, Pennsylvania. Four more Mollies were hanged in that same place that day. Forty miles away, at Mauch Chunk, four more Irishmen, dressed in new suits and each carrying one red rose, were hanged. Before the year was out, ten more Sons of Molly McGuire were hanged by their necks until they were dead. Nineteen men in all died because of the direct testimony of detective James McParlan.

And with them died the Molly McGuires.

The Mollies were no part of the union movement in the coal regions. But *what* they did and *why* they did it and the deaths of their leaders brought to light the terrible working conditions of the miners.

The result was that public opinion forced the mine owners to install some safety measures and to give the workers a little better pay.

It was as if a clean wind swept through the coal towns. Honest Irishmen again started small unions—unions that eventually combined and, in time, were able to make mine work respected and honored. (But the struggle of the young unions for recognition wasn't easy. The next chapter will describe the violent years before there was peace between the miner and his employer.)

Almost a hundred years have passed since "the Mollies" was a name to whisper, a name with which to frighten naughty children. But they are remembered.

People who grew up in those coal counties have heard many tales about the Mollies from their grandparents and great-grandparents. And sometimes, they'll tell you, with a quick glance over their shoulder, that often at night—when mists from the mines swirl around the yellow lights at street corners—they see shadowy figures, and even hear the beginning of a song:

*"How far is it to Pottsville, stranger,*
*did you say?"*
*"I guess it's about a dozen miles away.*
*"Straight out in that direction—over*
*the hill."*
*"Do the Mollies still lie in wait*
*to kill?"*

# 6 The Unions

A Boy's Vow

In the early evening of a June day in 1890 a young boy climbed down the steep steps of a coal breaker in the town of Lucas, Iowa, and stood looking at the rosy sunset.

He had seen the dawn that morning when he climbed the steps of the tall, grimy building in which coal was sorted into various sizes by many small hands. The dreary place did have some windows, but they were so stained with coal dust that only a few rays of sunlight fell on the streams of coal that flowed past the boy and dozens like him.

The boy was ten years old. His name was John Llewellyn Lewis.

He pushed back his cap with fingers that were black claws. Only the whites of his eyes showed in a face as dirty as the shirt he wore. As he watched the sun slip down behind mountains of coal slag and waste, he swore a vow: If he could, he would someday make the lives of miners better.

That same vow was in his heart and mind in 1920, when he was elected president of the United Mine Workers of America.

Since the first time one group of men paid for the muscle of another group to labor for profit, no worker had ever been so misused and exploited as had the miner. Few native-born Americans were willing to labor deep in the earth, in constant danger of being crippled or losing their lives for the small pay offered by mine owners. So the coal was dug chiefly by immigrants and especially by the Irish. These poor (and mostly ignorant) people were willing to work and live like animals for the opportunity of being in the great land of America.

But conditions like that couldn't continue. Beginning in the first half of the nineteenth century (even before the time of the Mollies), small groups of men began to try to form legal unions. They asked only a few simple things of the mine owners. First, that they be paid more than ten cents an hour; second, that the shantytowns be made cleaner; and third, that some safety measures be installed in the mines.

Those early struggling unions were failures. No matter how righteous their cause was, to the mine owners they were lawbreakers. Hired killers were brought into the mining fields, and many members of the unions were beaten, and some murdered. These "strike breakers" soon became as vicious as the Mollies would be. But the law was on their side, and nothing could be done to stop their cruelty. The name of every striker, and even the names of the friends of a striker, were put on a dreaded blacklist, and no mine owner would hire them.

## A UNION OF UNIONS

These small and isolated unions soon realized that they must combine into one organization if their pleas were to be heard. They met in groups on street corners, in private houses, and in churches, to listen to organizers, who told them again and again that it was better to have their names on a blacklist than to labor in deadly danger and watch their families starve. Collections were taken and even personal belongings pawned, so that the best speakers could travel from one mining field to another to spread the news of what fellow miners were doing and planning for the betterment of all.

But it wasn't easy to combine the many small unions into one that could speak for all. There were unions in the coalfields of the North, South, East, and West. A strike called in the coal regions of Pennyslvania had no effect on the mine owners in Illinois, and a strike of miners in Virginia had nothing to do with the operation of mines in Missouri.

With the advent of the Civil War, the activities of the unions almost stopped. Every mine was operating at full capacity to feed the industries that manufactured war materials. It was unpatriotic to strike, and those few unions that did try to stop work in some mines were forced to return to the pits by threats of violence and jail.

When the Civil War ended, the mines were producing more coal than the country needed in peacetime. The result was that many closed, and those that still operated could supply jobs for only a few men. Most of the unions had disbanded. The lives of the miners, present and future, appeared to be hopeless.

But there was a spark left alive. In 1868 the miners of Schuylkill County, Pennsylvania, formed the Benevolent Workingmen's Association. They proclaimed that "the miner must be rewarded for his dangerous labor, and must not any longer be made the victim of the operators' greed and speculation." Similar associations were formed in other mine fields.

Over the years many of these associations combined into two—the National Federation of Miners, with a man named Chris Evans as president, and the Knights of Labor, whose Grand Master Workman was named

Terence V. Powderly. But even then the miners didn't have the strength to fight successfully for their rights. *Complete* unity was the only way to meet the power of the mine owners.

And at last it happened.

On January 3, 1891, the two unions met at Columbus, Ohio. It was a cold day. Snow lay inches deep on the rutted streets. The breath of the horses that pulled the buggies hung in clouds of vapor in the chill air. Men in overcoats and muffled to their ears in scarves scrambled out of those buggies and entered the large meeting hall.

The speechmaking continued for a month. There were angry shouts, fist shakings, and even fights. But finally their one great need—unity—brought them together. On January 30 the two unions agreed to become one—the United Mine Workers of America. John B. Rae was its first president.

## EARLY DAYS OF THE UMWA

The new union would not be alone in its fight for the rights of its workers. Although it was a separate entity, dedicated to the betterment of the miners, it would also be a part of the American Federation of Labor. The federation, which had been organized in Pittsburgh, Pennsylvania, on November 15, 1881, then represented fifty thousand members belonging to small unions in the construction, electrical, and plumbing trades. Its original name was the Federation of Organized Trades and Labor Unions. In 1886 the name was changed to the American Federation of Labor.

The goals of the miners' union were these: no child labor; the honest weighing of coal (many miners' pay depended on the amount of coal they dug each day); more and better safety conditions; and, of great importance, the payment of their wages *in cash,* instead of credit at the "pluck me" stores.

Having only one big union helped in the fight for miners' rights, but it did not make the job easy. The

A company store                    *United Mine Workers of America*

frequent economic depressions, when mines were shut
down or worked only part-time, contributed to the dif-
ficulties of the struggle. But every year more miners
joined their union, and eventually it became strong
enough to force the mine owners to ease some of the
burdens of the workers.

Once, in those early years, the UMWA almost disappeared. During the depression of 1893—1896, when
many mines closed and others operated at half capacity,
some miners and their families actually starved to
death. But the majority survived. The miners helped
one another with food, shelter, and inspiration, and
kept their union alive.

In 1896, when William McKinley was elected the
twenty-fifth President of the United States on the slogan of "a full dinner pail for every worker," the miners
decided to act. One hundred and fifty thousand miners
went on strike in eleven states. It was time, they
thought, to get a "full dinner pail."

(The dinner pail was the companion of every workman in those days. Mines and factories had no

cafeterias or snack bars. The pail was made of tin and contained the worker's dinner, usually a couple of sandwiches and some fruit. Later a small thermos bottle was added for hot coffee or soup. Now most factories have facilities to feed their employees, but even today the miner who goes deep into the earth to dig coal still carries his dinner pail.)

The mine owners did their utmost to break the strike and wreck the union. Private police shot down pickets at the mine gates. In Latimer, Pennsylvania, twenty-four unarmed miners were killed.

Finally the newspapers of the country began to print stories of the outrages, and public opinion turned against the mine owners. That, and the fact that McKinley's election stopped the depression and revived the American industrial giant (thus creating a demand for more coal), made the owners agree to meet some of the demands of the union.

The time was ready for men like John Mitchell and John L. Lewis.

### JOHN MITCHELL

John Mitchell was born in Braidwood, Illinois, in 1870, within sight of the breakers of a local coal mine. Orphaned at six, he had little or no formal schooling. He didn't begin work as a breaker boy, as so many other mine leaders did, but lived on a farm. However, at the age of eleven he did enter the mines to do the labor of a full-grown man.

Before he was twenty he was taking an active part in the union movement. By the time he was twenty-seven he was secretary-treasurer of the Illinois branch of the United Mine Workers of America. One year later he was made head of the entire union.

His friends claimed he worked almost twenty-four hours a day. He traveled constantly, forging stronger and stronger links to bind the smaller unions to the UMW. The miners honored and respected him. In every speech he repeated these words: "The coal you dig isn't Irish or Welsh or English—it's just plain coal. And you must fight together for honest pay to mine that coal."

John Mitchell called many strikes and won most of them. Slowly the conditions improved under which the miners lived and worked. And for every improvement the miners and their families blessed John Mitchell.

But the hard work ruined his health, and in 1907 he retired as president of the union. He had increased its membership from 31,000 to 270,000 and was considered the greatest labor leader of his day.

During the next ten years other dedicated men led the United Mine Workers of America. Tom L. Lewis (no relation to John L.) followed Mitchell. Next were John P. White and Frank J. Hayes. Although these men worked hard, very few improvements were made in the lives of miners during their terms in office.

On May 16, 1910, the Congress of the United States created a Bureau of Mines. The mining of coal had become big business. Because ships, trains, and factories demanded more coal, it was logical that the government take an interest in an industry that was digging and selling one of the people's natural resources.

But the Bureau of Mines was of little help in bettering the conditions of the miners. It had no authority to force the mine owners to do anything except produce more coal. The mine owners were kings in an industry the entire country depended on for muscle. The labor force was expendable. Miners who were killed or maimed could be replaced. But a closed mine produced no coal.

The stage was set for the entrance of John L. Lewis. He stayed in the center of that stage for the next forty-nine years.

## JOHN L. LEWIS

Lewis was a breaker boy at ten, a miner at seventeen, and president of his local union at twenty-nine. He was self-educated and loved to study the classics. At union meetings his speeches were peppered with quotations from philosophy and history, and he held the miners spellbound.

Lewis was a forceful man. He had piercing eyes, a mop of black hair, and heavy black eyebrows that soon made him known throughout the world. He not only attracted attention, he forced people to look at and listen to him. In 1916 he became vice-president of the UMW. A few years later, in 1920, he was its president.

At the end of World War I the membership of the union had grown to 500,000, and there were millions of dollars in the union treasury. It was time, Lewis decided, to call a countrywide strike to win, once and for all, the rights the miners had been deprived of for so long.

It was a long and bitter strike, and the miners won. It was Lewis' first great victory. He had others over the years, but then came times of disappointments and defeats for his beloved miners.

After the Great War, more coal was being mined than the country's industries could use. Also, because Lewis' strikes had obtained more pay for the miners, many of the industries, especially the railroads and steel mills, began to open their own mines and hired only nonunion workers at lower pay. These were called captive mines, and many miners left their union to work in them. The percentage of miners who were union members dropped from 75 percent in 1922 to 14 percent in 1933.

It was a dark time for the United Mine Workers of America, and it soon became a dark time for all workers. In 1929 the country slipped into a depression, and thousands of factories and mills closed their doors.

But Lewis was a fighter. He was also convinced that this great country would begin to move forward again and that when it did the workers would need strong unions to obtain their fair share of the new prosperity.

His first concern was to rebuild the UMW. He traveled from one mining community to another, talking and pleading with the workers. And he convinced them again that only in union was there strength. In a few years the membership once more numbered 500,000.

But unionizing the miners wasn't enough for John L. Lewis. He began to think of the hundreds of thousands of workers in other industries who were without strong leadership. All he had to do was point to what he had accomplished for the miners, and these workers flocked to join him. In 1935 he was able to combine all these unions into the Committee of Industrial Organization—the CIO. The name was later changed to the Congress of Industrial Organization.

During those years Lewis was helped by Franklin D. Roosevelt, who had been elected the thirty-second President of the United States and who also believed that the only way workers could obtain fair wages was to belong to unions.

But this friendship didn't last long. President Roosevelt thought Lewis was calling too many strikes against industries, especially at a time when the country was trying to overcome a depression. At last, when the CIO called a strike against the steel companies, Roosevelt refused to help him.

The two men became open enemies when Roosevelt ran for a third term as President. Lewis vowed to do everything he could to defeat him, and even promised that if Roosevelt were elected, he would resign as president of the CIO.

Roosevelt was elected, and Lewis did resign. But he was still head of the United Mine Workers of America. And now he had the time to devote all his energies to their welfare.

The miners of coal, once the forgotten men of labor, became one of the highest paid. The vow Lewis had taken many years before, when he was a breaker boy, he made come true. He had made mistakes, many of them, but the miners were better off because of his leadership.

Lewis was loved, and he was hated. He was loved by the miners who were earning high wages, but he was hated by those who were unemployed. Lewis had won so many benefits for his miners that the owners were forced to raise the price of coal so high that many industries began to use other fuels—natural gas and oil.

Even though miners had now become the highest paid of American workmen, there was little happiness in the coalfields. So many mines were forced to shut down, and there were so many unemployed miners that some communities in the coal regions were like ghost towns.

John Llewellyn Lewis died at his home in Alexandria, Virginia, on June 11, 1969, aged eighty-nine years. Other men are leading, and will continue to lead, the United Mine Workers of America. But John L. Lewis will always be remembered by those who still go deep into the earth to dig the rock that burns. As one old miner told his friends when his huge hospital bill was paid by the UMW welfare fund, "You boys can pray to anyone you want to, but my saint is John L. Lewis."

# 7 How Coal Is Being Used Today

THE HEART OF COAL

A young scientist was talking to a group of students who were touring the research laboratory of one of our country's great coal producers. He held up a shining black object.

"In the heart of this piece of coal," he said, "there are more benefits to mankind than can be found in any other natural resource."

He picked up a jar that contained a thick black mass.

"This is tar," he explained, "just *one* of the by-products of coal. Look at those." He pointed to rows of more jars. "They hold more than three hundred different chemicals, and all are obtained from tar. Not only that, but each of those chemicals can be broken down into dozens of others."

It sounds fantastic, but it's true. Every chemical that has been discovered in coal leads on to others, and each of those new chemicals contains more and different substances. Among the products of such substances are aspirin, saccharine, paints, dyes, explosives, fertilizers, perfumes, mothballs, drugs, plastics, and hundreds of other useful materials.

But only a small amount of the coal being dug today is used solely to produce these chemicals. Most are obtained from the gases and tars that are given up by coal as it is burned.

### DIRECT SOURCE OF ENERGY

Although more and more experimentation with the by-products of coal has gone on over the past years, with marvelous results, the use of coal itself as a direct

Transmission lines and switchyard carry the electricity—"coal by wire"—from the modern Wabash River generating station of the Public Service Company of Indiana at Terre Haute. Pulverized coal can generate up to 521,000 kilowatts at this efficient station.

*Edison Electric Institute*

In the control room of Philadelphia's Electric Company's Eddystone electric generating station, two operators monitor the operation of automatic equipment throughout the plant. The Eddystone station, burning bituminous coal, generates 1.6 kilowatt hours for each pound of coal consumed, making it the world's most efficient power plant. Coal is the dominant fuel of the electric utility industry, producing more electricity than all other fuels combined.

*Philadelphia Electric Company*

source of energy has decreased. By the early 1970's, when the countries of the world were suddenly shocked into the realization that the oil and natural gas they had come to depend on would no longer be available in the near future, coal had almost been forgotten.

In the United States its production had fallen from 631 million tons a year in 1947 to less than 429 million tons. Each miner, who dug an average of sixteen tons a day in 1969, was producing only eleven tons. According to the United States' Bureau of Mines, at least 500 million tons must be mined annually simply to keep equipment and a labor force maintained.

But some farseeing men, the owners and operators of mines and the managers of many industries, had been sure all along that a time would come when coal would

The first coal pours into the stockpile of Potomac Electric Power Company's Chalk Point, Maryland, plant. The plant is designed to burn 1.5 million tons of coal a year, delivered by 100-car unit trains which are unloaded within a few hours. The coal is delivered to the 250,000-ton storage pile by the traveling boom, which can also reclaim coal from storage by its unique bucket wheel at the rate of 250–500 tons an hour. The stacker-reclaimer unit can be operated by remote control from the heart of the power plant, using closed-circuit television. The rake above the wheel breaks up the storage pile when coal is recovered.

*National Coal Association*

Coal-fired Big Sandy power plant of Kentucky Power Company at Louisa, Kentucky, has an unusual cooling tower. This electric generating station burns more than one million tons of coal a year.

*American Electric Power Corporation*

once again be used as the country's power source. Therefore, although trains and ships no longer burn coal for fuel, and only a small percentage of private houses are heated by coal furnaces and stoves, coal (mostly bituminous) is being dug and used for other purposes. The public utilities consume the largest proportion.

More than half the electricity generated in the United States comes from burning coal, and a great many houses use electricity for heating and cooling. A number of larger buildings—hotels, offices, hospitals, apartment complexes—that had converted to, or been built to use, oil and gas have reconverted to coal, and new buildings are often built with coal-burning furnaces as original equipment.

New methods of mining have lowered the cost of coal at the mine mouth. Great amounts of it are burned right there, and the coal gas produced is sent through pipes directly to commercial markets hundreds of miles from the mines. Coke, a principal by-product of coal, is being used in huge quantities by the steel, cement, paper, and chemical companies.

Much of the coal we mine today is exported. In fact, we are the world's largest exporters of coal. We ship an average of 20 million tons to Canada annually and more than 30 million tons to Europe. Even Japan buys an average of 10 million tons from us each year.

More than half our coal reserves lie untouched in the ground west of the Mississippi River. However, most of what we mine today still comes from the thick black veins of Appalachia and Pennsylvania.

About 1,200 small privately owned mines produce 40 percent of our coal. The remaining 60 percent comes from fifteen larger companies, of which Peabody Coal of St. Louis and Consolidated Coal of Pittsburgh are the largest. Only three of the fifteen giant companies—Pittston, North American, and Westmoreland—are independent. Six large companies are controlled by the petroleum interests; two captive mines (mines owned by the steel companies and whose workers are not members of the UMW) are operated by U.S. Steel and Bethlehem Steel.

So although most people have forgotten about the common black rocks, coal is still being mined and, more important, is still being experimented on. Not only have

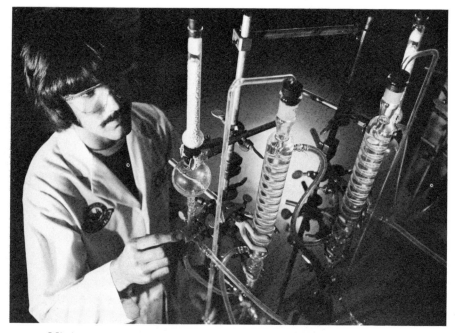

Mining engineer determining incombustible content of mine dust.
*Bituminous Coal Research, Inc.*

better methods been invented for digging and moving it to markets, but laboratories across the country are discovering more wonders in its black heart.

### Two Complex Compounds

Coal contains two completely different and complex parts. One is organic and is composed of carbons whose origin was once living plants. The second is inorganic and is made up of minerals in the earth's crust that became part of coal during the thousands of years of its formation. There are four principal methods of obtaining these substances.

*Carbonization* means baking coal in an airtight oven until two thirds of it has turned into coke. The other third of the coal becomes coal gas and the black tar that covers many of our roads. The gas is used as a fuel, but it also can be converted into hundreds of different chemicals. The tar can be broken down into other substances for various purposes.

*Hydrogenation* is a method of combining oil, hydrogen, and coal under tremendous heat and pressure and then separating the resulting mass into ethane, butane, and propane gases. From these are made benzine, aniline, and naphthalene. These substances are then changed into hundreds of useful things like paints, plastics, and perfumes. This process is the one being used now and with improvements will be extensively used in the future to make synthetic oils and gasoline. Variations of this method might eliminate our need for importing so much petroleum.

*Gas synthesis* is a process of developing chemicals from coal by oxidation. Pulverized coal is turned into a gas by exposing it to oxygen and very hot steam. This gas, a mixture of hydrogen and carbon monoxide, is then passed over various solid catalysts. (A catalyst is a substance that causes a chemical reaction in materials without undergoing any change itself.) In this process catalysts are usually bars of metal. If the catalyst is cobalt, the gas is changed into diesel fuel. If the catalyst is iron, the gas becomes gasoline.

*Gasification* is a method of burning coal *in the mine* to obtain a gas that can be piped directly to factories and mills to produce heat and power. This coal gas can also be converted into various light and heavy oils, and even gasoline.

## COAL GAS

The wonders that are hidden in common coal were not discovered easily. The secrets were slowly revealed over hundreds of years of experimentation. Coal can be compared to an onion. As one "layer" is peeled away, another appears. With coal there appears to be no end to the "layers."

Coal gas, which is being used in many places to take the place of natural gas, was discovered in Belgium in 1609 by Jan Baptista van Helmont, who wrote in his journal that "he had caught an elusive wild spirit" from heated coal. It was he who invented the name "gas." Helmont used his "elusive spirit" only to astonish his friends. Nothing was done about the possibilities of its everyday use until 1802, when a Scotsman named William Murdock lighted an entire factory with it. After Murdock's demonstration, chemists began to dream of lighting whole cities with gas.

But many laughed at the idea. "There's a madman proposing to light London with smoke!" So wrote Sir Walter Scott to a friend in 1812. But London *was* eventually illuminated with that strange "smoke," as were many other cities.

Coal gas, manufactured in immense coke ovens, was piped to where it could be used. The streets of the world's largest cities, including New York, were soon torn up so that pipes, many of wood, could be laid from coke ovens to the gaslights that stood on every corner. Thousands of lamplighters, men with long tapers, lighted those lamps every night.

In 1806 the home of David Melville in Newport, Rhode Island, presented an astonishing sight. This ingenious New Englander manufactured coal gas in his backyard and lighted his home and the street in front of it with bright gaslights. People came from long distances to sit in their carts and carriages and marvel at the display. Melville kept on experimenting and improving his gas-making ovens until at last he was lighting many of the cotton mills in New England. In 1817 he was given permission by the U.S. Government to provide the energy for one of America's oldest lighthouses—the Beaver Tail lighthouse on Narragansett Bay.

One spring night in Baltimore, Maryland, in the year 1816, a huge throng gathered outside the new studio of

Rembrandt Peale. Peale was one of the country's most famous portrait painters, and he had arranged a special attraction for that night. He had advertised in the newspapers that he would demonstrate the marvelous gaslights he had imported from Europe.

The display, which consisted of lighting the studio and the streets surrounding it, was such a success that on June 17, 1816, the city council of Baltimore passed an ordinance giving Peale and some friends the right "to make gas, lay pipes, and enter into a contract with the City of Baltimore to light all its streets." Peale's was the first gas company to operate commercially in the United States.

Coal gas is one of the simplest substances to make and is a basic experiment in modern chemistry. A small can is filled with bituminous coal, the lid pressed on tight, and a hole punched in the top to allow the gas to escape. When the can is placed on a burner, a smoky vapor rises from the hole. If a lighted match is placed at the hole, a steady flame results. As this vapor (coal gas) burns, a dark sticky liquid forms around the hole. This is coal tar. The coal in the can will eventually become a hard gray spongelike mass. This is coke.

Although relatively small amounts of coal gas are currently being used to create energy in our industries, more and more of this easily obtained fuel will be produced as the supply of natural gas diminishes. New ways of making it and using it will be described in the last chapter.

### OTHER BY-PRODUCTS

Two other important gases are now being manufactured by burning coal. One is "water gas," which is really a combination of two gases. This valuable vapor is formed when steam is forced through a bed of burning coals. The steam, reacting with the hot coal, forms hydrogen and carbon monoxide. The steam is forced through the coal until the mass cools to approximately

100 degrees Fahrenheit, when the gas-making process stops. Then the coal bed is made white-hot again by blowing air through it (creating a draft). When it reaches a sufficient heat, more steam is forced through it, and the process is repeated again and again. This combination of the two gases is said to be "lean," because it doesn't produce as much heat when burned as does coal gas. One of the benefits of water gas is that it can be regulated by adding other gases to it to produce fuels of various heating strengths.

"Producer gas" is a vapor made by passing cool air slowly through beds of burning anthracite. (Anthracite coal, remember, burns hotter than other types of coal, and is the only kind used in making producer gas.) The oxygen in the air and the carbon in the anthracite combine to make pure carbon monoxide. This gas, like water gas, is used with additives when a special degree of heat is needed, especially in experimentation.

One very important discovery of a coal by-product came in 1845, when benzine was separated from coal tar, the black liquid formed when coal gas is burned. Benzine not only is the source of nylon and similar products, but it, with several other coal chemicals, will be the basis for making the oils and gasoline that will free us from dependence on other countries.

Of the hundreds of chemicals we are now obtaining from coal, here is a list of a few, and some of the useful things we are manufacturing from them today:

1. *Creosote.* One of its uses is as a wood preservative. Telephone poles and other wood supports placed in the ground have a life of more than forty years when treated with it.

2. *Pitch.* This substance is used in roof construction and road paving, in various types of paints, in storage batteries, and in all kinds of insulation.

3. *Naphthalene.* Plastics, insecticides, fungicides, explosives, and even moth balls are made from it.

4. *Phenol.* This compound is used in medicines, detergents, perfumes, flavorings, varnishes, insecticides, and disinfectants.

5. *Cresol* and *cresylic acid.* These are used in disinfectants, plastics, and adhesives.

6. *Pyridine* and *picoline.* Medicines of all sorts— antiseptics, analgesics, antihistamines, and sulfa drugs—are made from these liquids.

7. *Ammonium sulfate.* This colorless salt is used in fertilizers and with other chemicals from which dozens of other useful things are manufactured.

8. *Anhydrous ammonia.* This chemical has many uses, among them processing gold and silver, making low-carbon steels, refining petroleum, and in the manufacture of refrigerants, plastics, textiles, and explosives.

9. *Ammonium nitrate.* This substance is used in manufacturing explosives and fertilizers.

10. *Nitric acid.* This corrosive liquid is used in explosives and in processing rare metals.

11. *Benzine.* One of coal's most versatile byproducts, benzine is used to produce synthetic rubber, nylon, plastics, medicines, dyes, explosives, photographic chemicals, solvents, fuel oil, and gasoline.

12. *Toluene.* This liquid is used in making aspirin, saccharine, paints, and lacquers, and is the last *T* in TNT—trinitrotoluene.

13. *Xylene.* This chemical is used in the manufacture of papers and cloth, protective coverings for ships and automobiles, sutures for surgery, and musical instruments. Gasoline and fuel oil are now being made with xylene.

14. *Sulfur.* Although this element is regarded as a hazard to our environment when it enters the air from the burning of bituminous coal, it is now being captured in various ways and used to make fungicides, insecticides, and sulfuric acid, from which dozens of other things are manufactured.

Coal gases and coal tars, the origins of these marvelous chemicals, come from burning coal. The gray spongelike mass that is left is coke. Although modern technology, spurred by the energy crisis, has found simpler and less wasteful ways of capturing coal gases and tars than by burning the black rocks, until the time when those new methods become common, coke ovens will continue to supply those materials.

Let's see how coke is made and how it is used.

# 8 Coke and Steel

## COKE OVEN

It could be a scene from Dante's Inferno. Grotesque figures move about in the semigloom. Sparks fly through the humid air. The heat is intense. There is a continuous roaring sound as piles of red-hot materials are dumped onto the floor or into waiting steel carts.

It is a modern coke oven in operation.

Without coke, there would be no steel, the backbone of our buildings, bridges, and thousands of other things that make our civilization what it is.

There is no doubt that primitive man used coke, but he didn't know how to make it. It is probable that he found chunks of the gray fuel in ancient coal beds that had been struck by lightning and then had smoldered for many years.

Probably he soon learned that these whitish rocks burned with a greater heat than the black lumps surrounding them, and must have considered himself lucky when he found a nest of them.

But it wasn't until thousands of years had passed that

95

people discovered that coke could be made by deliberately burning coal for a certain time, or until the gases had been removed. And it wasn't until many years later that they found that those gases could be converted into thousands of astonishing and useful things.

In 1771 the poet Goethe visited some coke ovens near Saarbrücken, Germany. Goethe was interested in everything, so when he learned that someone was making a gray substance that burned hotter than the coal it was made from, he had to see for himself.

The German poet was dismayed at the dirt and confusion he found. The overseer of the project, according to Goethe, was "a man worn, bent, haggard, and wearing ill-assorted clothing." Coke making is hard and dirty work. It must have been harder and dirtier two hundred years ago.

But the man did show the poet how ordinary coal, placed under pressure and burned, produced gases that could be distilled into a light oil and a heavy oily mass that was being used to grease cart wheels. (Before that time animal fat was spread on axles to make the wheels of carts and carriages turn easily.) The man was selling the light oil to local coal mines, where the miners burned it in the small lamps they attached to their hats to light their way through tunnels.

## A SPECIAL FUEL

From the beginning of the Industrial Revolution, when energy was first used to turn turbines, and for other purposes, people had been seeking a fuel that would burn steadily and give off intense heat. The search became of great importance.

At first wood was used. Then so much was needed (when it was discovered that charcoal made from it burned hotter than the original wood) that whole forests were cut down. Soon all the trees growing around factories were used up. Wood had to be hauled long distances, making it very expensive.

It has been estimated that five thousand acres of woodland would have had to be cut each year to provide for the production of iron, lead, and copper in England during the 1600's. Two hundred years later, as the Industrial Revolution got under way, that figure would be tripled. In America, as that revolution caught on, the vast forests along the eastern seaboard were fast disappearing as more and more ironworks used charcoal in their furnaces. Both England and America bought a newer and better fuel.

Coal, of course, had been known for some time, but it was used in fireplaces to heat rooms, especially in the homes of the rich. Mostly anthracite was used for that purpose (as it is today) because it was harder, burned longer, and gave off little smoke. But anthracite, lying deeper in the ground, was more expensive than ordinary bituminous coal.

Then some early experimenter discovered that if bituminous coal was "roasted," the gray lumps that were left could be forced into a heat even more intense than that which was produced by the expensive anthracite. All industries, from the brewing of beer to iron making, began to use the new wonder fuel. And so the coke oven was born.

### EARLY METHODS OF MAKING COKE

One of the early methods of making coke was the hearth process. Several tons of coal were piled in a pyramid shape on the ground. Then a layer of damp earth (damp to keep it firmly packed) was placed on the pile (like decorating a cake with icing). The coal was set on fire and left to smolder for at least a day. After water was sprayed over the pyramid and the dirt shoveled away, the result was coke—about one third the original amount of coal used.

Another method of coke making was introduced by an Englishman, John Wilkinson, in 1768. He erected a tall chimney of bricks and then piled coal around it. A fire was built in the chimney and the heat roasted the coal. This took a trifle longer than the pyramid method, but more coke could be made at one time, and the quality was better.

Coke became popular in England, Europe, and the United States, and those who were experienced in making it were in demand.

On April 8, 1813, the *Pittsburgh Mercury* carried this advertisement by a man named John Beal:

> To Proprietors of Blast Furnaces
> John Beal, lately from England, being informed that blast furnaces are in the habit of melting ore with charcoal, and knowing the great disadvantages it is to proprietors, is induced to offer his services to instruct them in the method of converting Stone Coal into Coak. The advantage in using Coak will be so great that it cannot fail of becoming popular if put into practice.

But the proprietors of foundries in America didn't rush to make use of "coak." It wasn't until five years after John Beal's advertisement that the first adventurous foundry owner began to burn the gray fuel.

One method of making coke was invented by a German alchemist named Johann Rudolf Glauber. It is carried out in a "beehive" oven—so called from its shape—and is still being used in many places today. Glauber wasn't interested in coke. What he wanted was coal tar, which he made from the gases given off by burning coal. He sold this tar by the bucketful to sailors to coat the bottom of their ships.

Glauber's beehive ovens were made of firebrick, and were about twelve feet in diameter and seven feet tall, with an arched roof exactly like a hive. The ovens were built in long rows, with retaining walls between them (as is done with all types of ovens) to capture as much heat as possible.

About six tons of coal are poured into each beehive oven through openings in its roof. If the ovens have been left to cool (during strikes, etc.), they must be carefully preheated before the coal is put in. However, if the operation of the ovens is continuous, the process can be repeated again and again. Air, to create a draft, is let into the ovens through side doors that can be regulated. As soon as the roasting process begins, gas rises from the surface of the coal and is captured as it emerges from small holes in the roofs. The coal is left to roast for two or three days. Then the coke is removed from doors in the fronts of the ovens. Coke produced this way is very hard, and the pieces are large.

### MAKING COKE TODAY

These ovens (like other types) are always located at steel-making plants, where the end product—coke—is to be used. The newest beehive ovens are 40 feet long, 13 feet high, and 2 feet wide. After crushed bituminous coal is dumped into them, they are heated to approximately 2000 degrees Fahrenheit. The heat is supplied by burning gas beneath the ovens (some of the same gas that is created by the roasting coal). It is the same principle as that behind the experiment with a can of coal on a kitchen burner. The ovens are large cans; the burning gas underneath is the stove.

After the coal has been roasted for the necessary time (depending on the type of coal or mixtures of coal used), the doors are opened, and the solid matter remaining is pushed or dumped onto the floor while it is still glowing with heat. Water is sprayed on it, and the result is a firm, porous gray substance—coke—that is almost 85 percent pure carbon.

Coke is an ideal fuel for use in the blast furnaces that make steel. It burns with a steady intense heat and also supplies carbon monoxide gas, an important ingredient in manufacturing steel of every hardness. And because of its firm structure, coke is strong enough to support the tremendous weight of iron ore and limestone that is placed on it in a blast furnace.

White hot coke being pushed from by-product coke ovens into a water-quencher car at U.S. Steel's Clairton Coke Works, Clairton, Pennsylvania.                    *U.S. Steel Corporation*

One of the new types of coke ovens is called the slot. A slot oven is a long, narrow brick chamber, with flues in the walls. The heat acting upon the coal can be carefully regulated, making the roasting produce different grades of coke as well as various types of gases.

In a slot oven the coal can be blended better than in a beehive oven. Various amounts of bituminous coal, lignite, and even anthracite can be used to produce coke of various types. Small slot ovens can convert four tons of coal into coke at one time; larger ovens can handle twenty tons. The large slot ovens are 40 feet long, 12 feet high, and 2 feet wide.

Another benefit of slot ovens is time. They can convert coal into coke in seventeen hours. Beehive ovens are less costly to construct, but the price of slot ovens is recovered by their efficiency.

No one in the steel or coal industries has been able to define exactly what a *quality* coke is. But all agree that some characteristics of the gray fuel should be uniform—size, structure, color, etc.—for the best results in blast and open-hearth furnaces. The best coke is high in carbon but low in moisture and sulfur. More than 70,000 tons of coke is produced each year, and that amount will almost double in the future.

### MAKING STEEL

Because coke and coal gases are so important in the manufacture of steel and because so much of these coal by-products is used for this purpose, the basic steel-making process should be explained.

First "pig iron" is made. This is done by heating a mixture of iron ore and limestone over a bed of burning coke. Without limestone, a gray rock consisting chiefly of calcium carbonate, there would be no iron and steel. When intense heat is applied to the mixture of ore and limestone, the calcium carbonate acts as a cleaner, absorbing the impurities in the ore, much as a blotter absorbs ink. The limestone becomes lime, and this, with the iron impurities, becomes *slag*. This mixture floats on top of the fluid iron and is drawn off repeatedly during the process.

After the slag has been separated from the mixture, what remains is pig iron, a pure liquid iron. When this iron becomes solid (by cooling), it is hard and brittle, but can support great weight. It has many uses, principally in engine blocks. If some slag (impurity from the smelting process) is added, it can be used decoratively as wrought iron because it then becomes malleable and can be shaped by hammering. Left pure, it becomes cast iron and is shaped by pouring or "casting" the liquid iron in molds. Most pig iron is manufactured in a *blast*

Tapping an open-hearth furnace at the Pittsburgh, California, works of the U.S. Steel's Columbia Steel Company. Heavier than slag, the molten steel flows from the furnace first, nearly filling the ladle. Slag follows next and is allowed to overflow into the slag pot to the right of the ladle.

*U.S. Steel Corporation*

furnace, so called because of the blasts of air forced through the coke to produce the necessary great heat.

Steel is usually produced in the United States in *open-hearth* furnaces. The name comes from the fact that the pool of liquid metal covered with a layer of slag lies on the hearth, or saucerlike floor, of the furnace, and is exposed to flames sweeping over it. In this method the slag absorbs even more impurities and the molten metal is *refined* into steel.

A modern open-hearth furnace might be 100 feet long and 25 feet wide. There is a door in front for charging (loading) the furnace with the mixture, and a tap in the rear through which the liquid steel flows from the furnace into a huge ladle. This tap hole is kept sealed with a special clay until the steel is ready for tapping.

Beneath the furnace are two *checker chambers,* so called because they are constructed of bricks arranged in a checkerboard pattern. They permit the alternate passage of air and exhaust gases.

Preheated air from one checker chamber enters at one end of the furnace, where it mixes with gas. This air-fuel mixture is blown into the furnace and burns with bright flames as it sweeps across the pool of metal on the hearth.

The hot exhaust gases pass out the other end of the furnace into the opposite checker chamber, where they heat the brickwork to a high degree. The direction of flow is changed every ten or fifteen minutes, so that while the brickwork in one chamber is being heated by the hot exhaust gases as they rush from the furnace, the hot bricks in the other chamber are heating the air that is entering the furnace.

When charging the furnace, limestone is put in first. Its purpose is the same as in the blast furnace—to remove some of the impurities and make slag. Next comes iron ore, then steel scrap, then liquid pig iron. The mixture will vary according to the kind of steel being made—more or less ore, more or less pig iron, more or less scrap, or scrap iron and steel of special kinds. It is exactly like mixing the ingredients when making various cakes. Different mixtures will produce different results.

The length of time these mixtures remain in the hearth furnaces is called the *refining* period. During this time the impurities in the ore and pig iron are carried away by gases or absorbed by the slag. As the flames from the air-fuel mixture sweep across the surfaces, the temperatures rise to approximately 2900 degrees Fahrenheit.

From time to time during the refining period samples are taken. These are rushed to the metallurgical laboratories for checking and analysis, so that the liquid steel can be tapped when it reaches the specifications for that particular batch being made.

## TAPPING THE FURNACE

The entire process of making a *heat* of steel might take eight to ten hours. When the steel has been refined to meet the formula desired, the furnace is tapped. The clay plug in the rear is punctured by a rocketlike explosive, and the hot steel gushes out in a fiery stream into the ladle. The slag, which leaves the furnace after the liquid steel, is collected in *slag pots* and saved for future heatings.

Most modern open-hearth furnaces produce from 150 to 375 tons of steel with each heat. After tapping, the furnace is charged again (perhaps with another kind of mixture to produce a different type of steel), and the process is repeated.

The liquid steel is poured from the ladle into ingot molds, where it cools and becomes solid. These ingots can be reheated and, with various alloys added, will produce a variety of still different types of steel. Some steel can be extruded (stretched) into wire as thin as a human hair. Other steel can be made so tough that it is used to construct battleships or the girders that form the skeleton of a skyscraper.

One of the newest methods of making very special kinds of steel is the electric arc furnace. Arc furnaces are lined with firebrick. When the furnaces are loaded or charged with various combinations of scrap, ore, limestone, and so on, large graphite electrodes are lowered into the mixture. Then enormous charges of electricity are sent through the electrodes. As the electricity arcs from one electrode to the other, a fierce heat is produced. The virtue of these furnaces is that the heat can be more carefully regulated than that in an open-hearth furnace, and thus they can produce a variety of special steels.

But whether heat is generated in beehive or slot ovens or electric furnaces, coal is required. In ovens it is necessary to make the coke that is burned to melt the mixtures. In electric furnaces coal is needed to make the electricity for the electrodes, either at the steel plant or at generating stations miles away.

One of the most important ingredients in making new steel is old steel and old iron. No matter how rusty the metal has become, it can be melted down, the impurities drawn off, and the rest converted into new steel.

Two main types of this scrap metal are used. Home scrap comes from the plant itself. For every ton of new steel produced, approximately three-quarter ton is finished steel. The remaining quarter ton is discarded because of imperfections and used again.

Purchased scrap comes from junk dealers, who collect secondhand steel and iron in any form. Obsolete machinery, old automobiles, railway cars and tracks, surplus or outdated military equipment are some of the scrap that eventually becomes part of new steel.

And so without coal, coke, and coal gases the steel industry would not be possible. From pins to palaces, from ships to shoes, our civilization depends on this gleaming metal, and the metal depends on the humble black rocks.

# **9** The Future of Coal

THE PROBLEMS WITH OIL, GAS,
AND NUCLEAR POWER

Coal is like Cinderella in the fairy tale. The dirty drudge—kept so long in a lowly place by the glamorous sisters, petroleum and natural gas, and by a stepmother that could be called nuclear power—is now being courted, petted, and appreciated.

When it became apparent that the reserves of petroleum and natural gas would be used up sooner than had been expected, it was of great importance that another source of energy be found, or our way of life would deteriorate rapidly. It wasn't that the estimates of the reserves of oil and natural gas had been wrong. It was because our use of those resources had multiplied and would multiply again and again.

Of course, over the years there had been experiments with other sources of energy, and some were in practical operation. A few kinds of nuclear power had been harnessed and put to work, in our ships, submarines, and electric-power stations. But still there was a fear of the

106

dreaded radiation that often accompanied the use of that power. Although no major accident had occurred at any nuclear installation, there was always the *chance* that, no matter how thorough the safety measures, some unforeseen incident might cause a catastrophe. Nuclear power could be likened to a ferocious beast in captivity. The cage and chains held the beast in check, but the danger was still there. A mistake on someone's part, a minor accident, and a fury might be released that could cause death and destruction.

And so, although nuclear power is being used, its future is in some doubt. Not only does it have the potential to endanger the lives of living things, but the by-products of its use—wastes, boiling waters poured into rivers, lakes, and oceans—can cause direct danger to our environment, and indirect danger to the whole chain of life.

### POTENTIAL NEW SOURCES OF ENERGY

There is also unlimited energy to be obtained from the sun; energy that will continue to pour over the earth until there no longer is an earth or a sun. But methods of using that source are still in their first faltering steps. Many private houses are now being heated and cooled by solar energy. But each installation is small and individual. The time will come when large amounts of the energy we use *for certain things* will be solar. But not yet.

There are potentials in other sources of energy that, like the rays of the sun, have been wasted or not understood. The power generated by the rising and falling of the tides is one. The wind is another. The heat generated by the earth's hot interior is still another. There are tremendous possibilities in these, but only years of study and experimentation will prove their value. Also in the future there may be sources of energy we can't even imagine today, just as a hundred years ago we couldn't have imagined radio or television.

But to realize all these future wonders, we must have

time. Time for our scientists to experiment. Time for them to think. Coal can buy us that time.

It has been estimated that our coal reserves will supply our needs for one or two thousand years. But that guess is based on *our current use.* If our use of coal is to be quadrupled or increased even more than that, our reserves will last a shorter time.

With the plans now in progress to expand the use of coal, to reconvert factories, buildings, and houses to burning the black rocks, even to make use of coal to create oil and gas, then the estimate of the time it would take to use what is still buried in the earth is about *four hundred years.*

But with the technology we have now, and will have, that should be time enough for our scientists to discover an infinite energy source.

### A Versatile Resource

It is fortunate that we have coal to fall back on, to take the place of other natural resources we have become accustomed to *and* the by-products of those resources that will soon disappear.

As we have seen, the by-products of atomic energy, instead of being of benefit to man, have the opposite effect. And, so far as we can see into the future, there are no by-products of solar, tidal, wind, or thermal power. But coal can not only be burned to create energy, it also produces more beneficial by-products than the energies it will replace. Not only can it replace the other power sources, but it can re-create the by-products of oil and natural gas.

Best of all, coal is a bargain fuel. Ships from all over the world sail to our shores to fill their holds with the precious cargo. In 1976 we sold $3.5 *billion* worth of it overseas.

Of course, as with everything else, the price of coal has increased. The cost of bituminous coal to industry is about seventeen dollars per ton. The special mixtures of

A rotary dumper tilts a hopper car of coal at the Chesapeake and Ohio Railway's coal piers at Newport News, Virginia. Coal is dumped onto a conveyor belt, which carries it along the pier for loading into the ship. Such high-capacity equipment allows the loading of 50,000-ton ships in a few hours.

*Chesapeake and Ohio Railway Company*

A river of coal flows along a conveyor belt to be loaded into a Great Lakes' freighter at the Chesapeake and Ohio Railway's Pier No. 4 at Presque Isle, Toledo, Ohio. Millions of tons of coal move through lake ports each year for shipment to Canada and U.S. ports in the Upper Midwest.

*Chesapeake and Ohio Railway Company*

coal used in making some types of steel might cost more than fifty dollars a ton. But it's still a bargain. Burning just eighty-one cents worth of coal will produce as much electricity as burning two dollars worth of oil.

### NEW PROBLEMS WITH COAL, NEW SOLUTIONS
But the coal that is to take the place of petroleum and

A self-unloading ship takes on a cargo of coal at the Bessemer and
Lake Erie Railroad Company's coal storage and transfer terminal at
Conneaut, Ohio. Coal bound for markets in Canada or for U.S. ports
on the upper Great Lakes arrives in rail cars, which are dumped in
an unloading shed. The coal is carried by conveyor belt to storage
piles (top left). When a ship is ready to load, the coal is recovered by
specialized equipment and carried by an outbound conveyor to a
surge bin (center), thence to a ship loader equipped with a telescopic
coal chute which distributes it evenly in the vessel's cargo holds.
*Bessemer and Lake Erie Railroad Company*

natural gas and give our scientists time to develop a permanent and infinite source of energy still lies in the ground. It has to be mined and moved to market.

That will take time, but not as much as was once thought. As more mines are reopened, more of the latest equipment will be needed to operate them. And that additional equipment *will* be made. Our industrial strength is accustomed to meeting the needs of any emergency. It has proved that often when, in a very short time, it has been able to convert from peacetime manufacturing to turning out planes, ships, and other war materials. And if, as our government has stated, our energy fight is as serious as being at war, it can do it again.

We are also fortunate in having scientists who foresaw the future need for coal and prepared for it. While some scientists (as described in a previous chapter) were discovering more and better ways to use coal by-products to improve our way of life, others were concentrating on methods of overcoming some of the drawbacks of coal when it is burned as fuel. One of those drawbacks has been sulfur.

When bituminous coal is burned, sulfur dioxide escapes with the gases, and too much of that compound can be a serious health hazard. However, the coal scientists have been working to eliminate that danger.

In some electric-generating stations, tall smoke stacks have been installed that soar more than a thousand feet into the sky. When sulfur dioxide is discharged at that height, it mixes with clean air and is harmless.

At Bituminous Research, Inc. (a part of the National Coal Association),scientists have developed a method whereby sulfur dioxide is converted into sulfur trioxide and then into sulfuric acid, a chemical from which fungicides, insecticides, and other useful things are manufactured.

The Pittsburgh and Midway Coal Mining Company, a

subsidiary of Gulf Oil Company, has succeeded in perfecting a method whereby pulverized coal is placed in a solvent (made from coal) and, after high heat and pressure has been applied, is converted into a liquid which, when cooled, becomes a black solid. This substance can then be pulverized again and burned, or melted and used like petroleum—with most of the sulfur trioxide removed.

At the University of Tennessee scientists have succeeded with a method by which coal can produce 50 percent more power from each ton, and capture 95 percent of sulfur dioxide. The method, which is called magnetohydrodynamics, was invented by the English scientist Michael Faraday in 1831. His theory had never been tried because it called for combustion temperatures as high at 5000 degrees Fahrenheit. Temperatures even higher are now possible, and Faraday's theory has proved to be correct.

The Faraday method produces electricity in two ways. Pulverized coal that has been treated with potassium is put into a combustion chamber and burned at 5000 degrees Fahrenheit or more. The expanding coal gases, ionized by the potassium, are forced at tremendous speeds through a pipe to a magnetic field. The high speed creates electricity, which is picked up from the flowing gases by conducting tubes. The steam created is then sent to turn conventional turbines and produces more electricity.

The method most in use now (and techniques are continually being improved) to remove sulfur dioxide is the "scrubber," whereby gases are treated with an absorbent before being sent up the smokestacks. At the Paddy's Run station of the Louisville Gas and Electric Company, the scrubbers remove 90 percent of the sulfur dioxide. At the Commonwealth Edison station in Chicago, scrubbers are able to take out eighty percent of the harmful gas before it is sent into the air. Even more efficient methods will soon be put to work in almost all the coal-burning units throughout the country.

### COAL TO OIL, COAL TO GAS

But what is being done to convert coal into petroleum, one of the principal reasons we are relying on the black rock in our energy war? A great deal is being done.

One of the processes being put forward by the Office of Coal Research is called Project COED. One plant now in operation at Princeton, New Jersey, can convert 36 tons of coal a day into 30 barrels of fuel. Since 1970 it has processed more than 5000 tons. That synthetic crude oil has been successfully tested by the U.S. Navy in its destroyers.

Another process is Project Clean Fuels from Coal, which originated with the Consolidation Coal Company, a subsidiary of Standard Oil of Ohio. This method will process 900 tons of coal a day, making 500 tons of clean-burning solid fuel *and* 600 barrels of distillate fuel, or, eliminating the solid fuel, will produce 2,600 barrels of distillate oil every day.

Gulf Research and Development Company has announced a process that will convert one ton of coal into three barrels of oil.

These are only a few of the dozens of coal-to-oil projects being developed today. The gasoline manufactured from this synthetic oil has now been reduced almost to equal the cost of gasoline made from petroleum. It is estimated by the Office of Coal Research that in a few years gasoline from coal will be cheaper than the fuel used in automobiles today.

Coal gas has also been successfully transformed into a substitute for natural gas. The Office of Coal Research, in partnership with the American Gas Association, is already manufacturing 1.5 cubic feet of pipeline gas each day in a Chicago plant. And a plant operated by Consolidated Coal Company, at Rapid City, South Dakota, is converting lignite to pipeline-quality gas. Other coal, oil, and gas companies are experimenting with using a mixture of coal gas and natural gas in the pipelines that service industries and private houses.

Under a contract with the Office of Coal Research, Bituminous Coal Research, Inc., is not only improving present methods of coal gasification but discovering better processes.

One is a two-stage gasifier. This coal reactor contains two stages of gasification in one unit. In one part pulverized coal is reacted with steam to produce methane gas (one of the principal parts of natural gas). The coal that remains, called char, is sent to another part of the unit, where it is combined with oxygen to produce a variety of gases. The goal of this method is eventually to produce a coal-methane gas that can compete in quality and price with natural gas.

### MOVING THE COAL TO MARKET

But still coal must be moved as quickly as possible from the mines to where it is to be used. Improvements have been made and will continue to be made in this area too. In some places "unit" trains—sometimes a hundred cars in length—move directly from mines to electric-generating plants. The trains stop only for servicing and fresh crews. They take on their loads while moving under chutes at the mine, then dump the coal at power plants while only slowing down. This method cuts the cost of coal almost in half.

One strip mine in Ohio has improved even on the unit train. Two fifteen-car trains (each car carrying 100 tons of coal) move slowly under loading chutes. Then, without a crew, they speed fifteen miles to a power station, dump their loads without stopping, and return to the mine to be loaded again. The trains are controlled both ways by automatic radio signals.

Another method that has been proving successful is to pulverize coal at the mines and pump it through pipelines directly to electric generators. A similar process is the "slurry" pipeline. This works like a toilet,

A unit coal train of one hundred or more cars is readied for departure from a coal preparation plant for a high-speed run directly to an electric utility plant or other large consumer. Such trains, loaded with 10,000 tons or more of coal in a few hours and unloaded with equal speed on the receiving end, have resulted in freight rate reductions of almost one half, making coal more competitive with other fuels. This preparation plant is at Humphrey No. 7 mine of the Christopher Coal Company, a subsidiary of Consolidation Coal Company at Osage, West Virginia. The plant also processes coal from another big mine nearby, delivered by the conveyor belt at right rear, and loads the coal into barges on the Monongahela River in the foreground.

*Consolidation Coal Company*

with the mixture of water and coal being "flushed" to the turbines. Although first used in London in 1914, the method is new here. One "slurry" pipeline, the Black Mesa Line, carries the coal-water mixture 273 miles from Kayenta, Arizona, to the Mohave Generating Station in southern Nevada.

Other, longer slurry lines are being built. One—1030 miles in length—will soon carry 25 million tons a year from the Wyoming mines of the Peabody Coal Company to the Middle South Utilities System in White Bluff, Arkansas. Another line, 1100 miles long, will carry slurry from Craig, Colorado, to Houston, Texas.

Other systems are being tried that will bring markets to the coal instead of coal to the markets. This is done by burning coal directly at the mine entrances and sending the electricity over high-power lines to where it is needed. Much of this is being done in western Pennsylvania, where the mines, using 500,000-volt lines, send power as far away as New York City. In the Four Corners area of New Mexico, power lines carry electricity directly from the mines to consumers in southern California.

### CONTINUING RESEARCH

The only part of coal for which formerly there was no use was ash—what was left after the black rocks had been completely consumed. But now scientists are discovering ways to make use of that once worthless remainder. West Virginia University's Coal Research Bureau has found a way to manufacture bricks, concrete blocks, and paving materials from coal ashes. This is of great benefit to power stations that burn coal to generate electricity, for now they can recover a sizable amount of the cost of the coal by selling the ashes.

Every country that has deposits of bituminous coal is searching for new ways (and improving old methods) of using that almost forgotten resource to take the place of natural gas and petroleum.

Rotary cement kilns turning at high speed at the plant of the Lawrence Cement Company, near Philadelphia. The cement industry consumes more than ten million tons of bituminous coal every year.
*Courtesy Benton and Bowles, Inc.*

The United States has an important advantage over most of these countries, because not only is our government making every effort to further coal research, it is also encouraging private organizations and universities to work toward the same goal. In other countries almost all experimentation is done by the government, often with great inefficiency and waste.

In the United States the Department of the Interior's Bureau of Mines, the Office of Coal Research, and the federal Energy Research and Development Administration not only conduct their own researches, but check and oversee the work being done by private foundations and universities.

At Morgantown, West Virginia, experiments are being carried out on coal-fired gas turbines and low-temperature tars. At Denver, Colorado, the carbonization of Western coals is being studied. At Grand Forks, North Dakota, lignite is being investigated for possible conversion to liquid fuels and gas. At Seattle, Washington, scientists are trying to find faster and better ways to prepare coal for market. At Juneau, Alaska, the coal resources of the north are being investigated with the aim of opening new mines. New oil is now flowing south through the Alaskan pipeline, but if coal can be used to its full potential, that oil, and most of our other oil and natural gas, can be saved and used for the very special work only oil or gas can do.

We should keep in mind that, regardless of the benefits we get from coal chemicals, coal itself is a fuel ready to be used. Coal is ready *now* to make electricity and to heat our homes, buildings, and factories. But will it last much longer than the oil and gas it is to replace? Four hundred years is not a long time, planetwise.

It must be remembered that the present estimate of our coal reserves—even if we multiply and then multiply again the amount we are now producing—is based on *known* reserves. There has been very little exploration for new coal. If, in the future, such exploration is carried out with the same vigor as the search for new oil and gas reserves, it is to be expected that new beds will be discovered.

The end of the benefits we can obtain from coal is not yet in sight, for there still are undiscovered secrets in the heart of this amazing black rock.

# Index